The Picture of Redemption in the Feasts of the Messiah

Dr. G. Michael Saunders, Sr.

This book is dedicated to my wonderful, loving wife, Patricia (Patty) Ann Straley Saunders, on the occasion of our 25th anniversary year. I praise the Lord for bringing us together. I love you.

Table of Contents

Preface

The Holidays of God that were given to the people at Mt. Sinai and recorded for us in Leviticus 23 are Biblical Holidays. God commands these and the people of Israel celebrate them or remember them even to this day. However there are also national holidays that the Jewish people celebrate that were not commanded by God. Some of them are in the Bible and some are not. But these are still considered to be very important holidays to the people. Some of them are mentioned in the New Testament in reference to Jesus and the teachings and miracles that He gave on those days.

Far from forbidding these, God does allow His people to celebrate and enjoy these holidays. And though not commanded by God these holidays do focus on God and center around the worship of God. These are not secular holidays because they are all about our love for God and His love for us.

This is also true in the church. The Christian Church has two holidays that span the entire Christian world – Christmas and Easter. Advent is a season of the year that leads into Christmas and is often consider part of the Christmas holidays instead of a separate holiday. These holidays are centered on the life of Jesus Christ and what He did to give us salvation. These holidays focus on His worship. They also cause us to look to the future toward His second coming and our eternal life with Him. Though these two holidays have been horribly commercialized and abused, for the Christian Church and for Christian families and individuals they are still always and only about the Lord Jesus Christ. So we delight in celebrating them.

This book covers all three of these kinds of holidays. Some are commanded by God, some are national holidays for the Jews and some are the holidays of the church. The previous book on this subject covered the Holidays of God found in Leviticus 23. This book covers all the rest of the holidays of God's people. The key truth in all of these holidays is that they point to and demonstrate the redemption that God has given to us through His Son our Savior Jesus Christ.

It is important to remember that these holidays find their joyous fulfillment in proclaiming the presence of God in our lives. So we must keep them Christ-centered in all their parts and experience them in such a way that we draw closer to God Himself. Then these Holidays of God have been well and truly celebrated!

Chapter One – Shabbat and Sunday
The Sabbath and the Lord's Day

"Remember the Sabbath day, to keep it holy. Six days you shall labor and do all your work, but the seventh day is a Sabbath of the LORD your God; in it you shall not do any work, you or your son or your daughter, your male or your female servant or your cattle or your sojourner who stays with you. For in six days the LORD made the heavens and the earth, the sea and all that is in them, and rested on the seventh day; therefore the LORD blessed the Sabbath day and made it holy." *(Exodus 20:8-10)*

After the Sabbath, at dawn on the first day of the week, Mary Magdalene and the other Mary went to look at the tomb. There was a violent earthquake, for an angel of the Lord came down from heaven and, going to the tomb, rolled back the stone and sat on it. His appearance was like lightning, and his clothes were white as snow. (Matthew 28:1-3)

When Jesus rose early on the first day of the week, he appeared first to Mary Magdalene, out of whom he had driven seven demons. (Mark 16:9)

Mary Magdalene went to the disciples with the news: "I have seen the Lord!" And she told them that he had said these things to her. On the evening of that first day of the week, when the disciples were together, with the doors locked for fear of the Jews, Jesus came and stood among them and said, "Peace be with you!" After he said this, he showed them his hands and side. The disciples were overjoyed when they saw the Lord. (John 20:18-20)

I, John, your brother and companion in the suffering and kingdom and patient endurance that are ours in Jesus, was on the island of Patmos because of the word of God and the testimony of Jesus. On the Lord's Day I was in the Spirit, and I heard behind me a loud voice like a trumpet, which said: "Write on a scroll what you see and send it to the seven churches: to Ephesus, Smyrna, Pergamum, Thyatira, Sardis, Philadelphia and Laodicea." (Revelation 1:9-11)

"For the Son of Man is Lord of the Sabbath." Matthew 12:8

The Sabbath
For six days, work is to be done, but the seventh day is a Sabbath of rest, holy to the LORD. Whoever does any work on the Sabbath day must be put to death. The Israelites are to observe the Sabbath, celebrating it for the generations to come as a lasting covenant. It will be a sign between me and the Israelites forever, for in six days the LORD made the heavens and the earth, and on the seventh day he abstained from work and rested.' " *(Exodus 3:15-17)*

The Nature of the Sabbath
The Sabbath (or Shabbat, as it is called in Hebrew) is the only feast of Israel that is mentioned in the Ten Commandments (1). It is also one of the best known and least understood of all Jewish observances. People who do not observe the Sabbath think of it as a day filled with stifling restrictions, or as a day of prayer like the Christian Sabbath.

But to those who observe the Sabbath, it is a precious gift from God, a day of great joy eagerly awaited throughout the week, a time when we can set aside all of our weekday concerns and devote ourselves to higher pursuits. In Jewish literature, poetry and music, the Sabbath is described as a bride or queen, as in the popular Shabbat hymn Lecha Dodi Likrat Kallah (Come, my beloved, to meet the Sabbath bride). It is said, "more than Israel has kept Shabbat, Shabbat has kept Israel (2)."

The Sabbath is the most important ritual observance in Judaism. It is the only ritual observance instituted in the Ten Commandments. It is also the most important special day, even more important than Yom Kippur. This is clear from the fact that more opportunities for congregants to be called up to the Torah are given on the Sabbath than on any other day.

The Sabbath is primarily a day of rest and spiritual enrichment. The word "Sabbath" comes from the root Shin-Beit-Tav, meaning to cease, to end, or to rest. The Sabbath is *not* specifically a day of prayer. Although the Jewish people do pray on the Sabbath, and spend a substantial amount of time in the synagogue praying, prayer is not what distinguishes the Sabbath from the rest of the week. Observant Jews pray every day, three times a day. To say that the Sabbath is a day of prayer is no more accurate than to say that the Sabbath is a day of feasting: the Jews eat every day, but on the Sabbath, they eat more elaborately and in a more leisurely fashion. The same can be said of prayer on the Sabbath (3).

Remember and Observe

In modern America, we take the five-day workweek so much for granted that we forget what a radical concept a day of rest was in ancient times. The weekly day of rest has no parallel in any other ancient civilization. In ancient times, leisure was for the wealthy and the ruling classes only, never for the serving or laboring classes. In addition, the very idea of rest each week was unimaginable (4). The Greeks thought the Jewish people were lazy because they insisted on having a "holiday" every seventh day.

The Sabbath involves two interrelated commandments: to remember the Sabbath, and to observe the Sabbath. First to remember, *"Remember the Sabbath day to sanctify it (Exodus 20:8).* We are commanded to remember the Sabbath, but remembering means much more than merely not forgetting to observe Shabbat. It also means to remember the significance of the Sabbath, both as a commemoration of creation and as a commemoration of the Hebrews freedom from slavery in Egypt.

In Exodus 20:11, after the Fourth Commandment is first instituted, God explains, *"because for six days, the Lord made the heavens and the earth, the sea and all that is in them, and on the seventh day, he rested; therefore, the Lord blessed the Sabbath day and sanctified it."* By resting on the seventh day and sanctifying it, we remember and acknowledge that God is the creator of heaven and earth and all living things. We also emulate the divine example, by refraining from work on the seventh day, as God did. If God's work can be set aside for a day of rest, how can we believe that our own work is too important to set aside temporarily?

In Deuteronomy 5:15, while Moses reiterates the Ten Commandments, he notes the second thing that we must remember on the Sabbath: *"remember that you were a slave in the land of Egypt, and the Lord, your God brought you forth from there with a mighty hand and with an outstretched arm; therefore the Lord your God commanded you to observe the Sabbath day."* What does the Exodus have to do with resting on the seventh day? It's all about freedom. As I said before, in ancient times, leisure was confined to certain classes; slaves did not get days off. Thus, by resting on the Sabbath, we are reminded that we are free. But in a more general sense, the Sabbath frees us from our weekday concerns, from our deadlines and schedules and commitments. During the week, we are slaves to our jobs, to our creditors, to our need to provide for ourselves; on the Sabbath, we are freed from these concerns, much as our spiritual ancestors were freed from slavery in Egypt.

These two meanings of Sabbath are remembered among the Jewish people when they recite Kiddush (the prayer over wine sanctifying the Sabbath or a holiday). The Friday night Kiddush refers to the Sabbath as both a memorial of the work of God in the beginning and a remembrance of the Exodus from Egypt.

The second theme is to Observe. *Observe the Sabbath day to sanctify it* (Deuteronomy 5:12). Of course, no discussion of the Sabbath would be complete without a discussion of the work that is forbidden on the Sabbath. This is another aspect of the Sabbath that is grossly misunderstood by people who do not observe it.

Most Americans see the word "work" and think of it in the English sense of the word: physical labor and effort, or employment. Under this definition, turning on a light would be permitted, because it does not require effort, but a Rabbi would not be permitted to lead Sabbath services, because leading services is his employment. Jewish law prohibits the former and permits the latter. Many Americans therefore conclude that Jewish law doesn't make any sense.

The problem lies not in Jewish law, but in the definition that Americans are using. The Torah does not prohibit "work" in the 20th century English sense of the word. The Torah prohibits "melachah" (Mem-Lamed-Alef-Kaf-Hei), which is usually translated as "work," but does not mean precisely the same thing as the English word. Before you can begin to understand the Sabbath restrictions, you must understand the word "melachah."

This is the kind of work that is creative, or that exercises control or dominion over your environment. The word may be related to "melekh" (king; Mem-Lamed-Kaf). The quintessential example of melachah is the work of creating the universe, which God ceased from on the seventh day. Note that God's work did not require a great physical effort: he spoke, and it was done.

The word "melachah" is rarely used in scripture outside of the context of the Sabbath and holiday restrictions. The only other repeated use of the word is in the discussion of the building of the sanctuary and its vessels in the wilderness (Exodus 31: 35-38). Notably, the Sabbath restrictions are reiterated during this discussion (Exodus 31:13), and thus we can infer that the work of creating the sanctuary had to be stopped for the Sabbath. From this, the Rabbis concluded that the work prohibited on the Sabbath is the same as the work of creating the sanctuary. They found 39 categories of forbidden acts (5). These are: sowing, plowing, reaping, binding sheaves, threshing, winnowing, selecting, grinding, sifting, kneading, baking, shearing wool, washing wool, beating wool, dyeing wool, spinning, weaving, making two loops, weaving two threads, separating two threads, tying, untying, sewing two stitches, tearing, trapping, slaughtering, flaying, salting meat, curing hide, scraping hide, cutting hide up, writing two letters, erasing two letters, building, tearing a building down, extinguishing a fire, kindling a fire, hitting with a hammer, taking an object from the private domain to the public, or transporting an object in the public domain.

All of these tasks are prohibited, as well as any task that operates by the same principle or has the same purpose. In addition, the rabbis have prohibited handling any implement that is intended to perform one of the above purposes (for example, a hammer, a pencil or a match) unless the tool is needed for a permitted purpose (using a hammer to crack nuts when nothing else is available) or needs to be moved to do something permitted (moving a pencil that is sitting on a prayer book), or in certain other limited circumstances. Objects that may not be handled on the Sabbath are referred to as "muktzeh," which means, "that which is set aside," because you set it aside (and don't use it unnecessarily) on the Sabbath (6).

Other Prohibitions

The Rabbis have also prohibited travel, buying and selling, and other weekday tasks that would interfere with the spirit of the Sabbath. The use of electricity is prohibited because it serves the same function as fire or some of the other prohibitions, or because it is technically considered to be "fire."

The issue of the use of an automobile on the Sabbath, so often argued by non-observant Jews, is not really an issue at all for observant Jews. The automobile is powered by an internal combustion engine, which operates by burning gasoline and oil, a clear violation of the Torah prohibition against kindling a fire. In addition, the movement of the car would constitute transporting an object in the public domain, another violation of a Torah prohibition, and in all likelihood the car would be used to travel a distance greater than that permitted by Rabbinical Prohibitions. For all these reasons, and many more, the use of an automobile on the Sabbath is clearly not permitted. As with almost all of the commandments, all of these Sabbath restrictions can be violated if necessary to save a life.

A Sabbath Celebration with the Lord Jesus – Luke 4:16-21

He went to Nazareth, where he had been brought up, and on the Sabbath day he went into the synagogue, as was his custom. And he stood up to read. The scroll of the prophet Isaiah was handed to him. Unrolling it, he found the place where it is written: "The Spirit of the Lord is on me, because he has anointed me to preach good news to the poor. He has sent me to proclaim freedom for the prisoners and recovery of sight for the blind, to release the oppressed, to proclaim the year of the Lord's favor." Then he rolled up the scroll, gave it back to the attendant and sat down. The eyes of everyone in the synagogue were fastened on him, and he began by saying to them, "Today this scripture is fulfilled in your hearing." (See Appendix #1 for a typical "practicing Jewish" Sabbath day today.)

The Lord's Day

In him you were also circumcised, in the putting off of the sinful nature, not with a circumcision done by the hands of men but with the circumcision done by Christ... Therefore do not let anyone judge you by what you eat or drink, or with regard to a religious festival, a New Moon celebration or a Sabbath day. These are a shadow of the things that were to come; the reality, however, is found in Christ. Colossians 2:11,16-17

The Nature of the Lord's Day – "the Fundamental Feast Day"

The Lord's Day, as Sunday was called from Apostolic times (Rom. 1:10), has always been accorded special attention in the history of the Church because of its close connection with the very core of the Christian mystery (7). In fact, in the weekly reckoning of time Sunday recalls the day of Christ's Resurrection. It is *Easter* that returns week by week, celebrating Christ's victory over sin and death, the fulfillment in Him of the first creation and the dawn of "the new creation" (2 Corinthians 5:17). It is the day which recalls in grateful adoration the world's first day and looks forward in active hope to "the last day", when Christ will come in glory (Acts 1:11; 1 Thessalonians 4:13-17) and all things will be made new (Revelation 21:5).

The Resurrection of Jesus is the fundamental event upon which Christian faith rests (1 Corinthians 15:14). It is an astonishing reality, fully grasped in the light of faith, yet historically attested to by those who were privileged to see the Risen Lord. It is a wondrous event which is not only absolutely unique in human history, but which lies at the very heart of the mystery of time. In fact, all time belongs to Christ and all the ages. Therefore, in commemorating the day of Christ's Resurrection not just once a year but every Sunday, the Church seeks to indicate to every generation the true fulcrum of history, to which the mystery of the world's origin and its final destiny leads. For Christians, Sunday is "the fundamental feast day", established not only to mark the succession of time but also to reveal time's deeper meaning.

The fundamental importance of Sunday has been recognized through two thousand years of history. Every seven days, the Church celebrates the Resurrection. This is a tradition going back to the Apostles, taking its origin from the actual day of Christ's Resurrection — a day thus appropriately designated "the Lord's Day".

From the Sabbath to Sunday

Because the Third Commandment depends upon the remembrance of God's saving works and because Christians saw the definitive time inaugurated by Christ as a new beginning, they made the first day after the Sabbath a festive day, for that was the day on which the Lord rose from the dead.

The mystery of Christ is the full revelation of the mystery of the world's origin, the climax of the history of salvation and the anticipation of the eschatological fulfillment of the world. What God accomplished in Creation and wrought for His People in the Exodus has found its fullest expression in Christ's Death and Resurrection, though its definitive fulfillment will not come until Christ returns in glory. In Him, the spiritual meaning of the Sabbath is fully realized, as Saint Gregory the Great declares: "For us, the true Sabbath is the person of our Redeemer, our Lord Jesus Christ"(8).

This is why the joy with which God, on humanity's first Sabbath, contemplates all that was created from nothing, is now expressed in the joy with which Christ, on Easter Sunday, appeared to His disciples, bringing the gift of peace and the gift of the Spirit (John 20:19-23). It was in the mystery of Christ that humanity, and with it the whole creation, "groaning in birth-pangs until now" (Romans 8:22), came to know its new exodus into the freedom of God's children who can cry out with Christ, "Abba, Father!" (Romans 8:15; Galatians 4:6). In the light of this mystery, the meaning of the Old Testament precept concerning the Lord's Day is recovered, perfected and fully revealed in the glory that shines on the face of the Risen Christ (2 Corinthians 4:6). We move from the "Sabbath" to the "first day after the Sabbath", from the seventh day to the first day: the *day of Dominion* becomes the *day of Christ*!

The Weekly Easter

It is clear that, although the Lord's Day is rooted in the very work of creation and even more in the mystery of the biblical rest of God, it is nonetheless to the Resurrection of Christ that we must look to in order to understand fully the Lord's Day. This is what the Christian Sunday does, leading the faithful each week to ponder and live the event of the Resurrection, the true source of salvation.

To "Keep Holy" by "Remembering"

The commandment by which God decrees the Sabbath observance is formulated in the Book of Exodus in a distinctive way: *"Remember the Sabbath day in order to keep it holy" (20:8)*. And the inspired text goes on to give the reason for this, recalling as it does the work of God: *"For in six days the Lord made heaven and earth, the sea, and all that is in them, and rested on the seventh day; therefore the Lord blessed the Sabbath day and made it holy" (v. 11)*. Before decreeing that something be done, the commandment urges that something be remembered. It is a call to awaken remembrance of the grand and fundamental work of God that is creation, a remembrance that must inspire the entire religious life of man and then fill the day on which man is called to rest.

The theme of remembering God's wonders is found also in the Book of Deuteronomy (5:12-15), where the precept is grounded less in the work of creation than in the work of liberation accomplished by God in the Exodus: *"You shall remember that you were a slave in the land of Egypt, and the Lord your God brought you out from there with mighty hand and outstretched arm; therefore the Lord your God commanded you to keep the Sabbath day" (Deuteronomy 5:15).*

Therefore, the main point of the precept is not just any kind of *interruption* of work, but the *celebration* of the marvels that God has wrought. Insofar as this remembrance is alive, full of thanksgiving and of the praise of God, human rest on the Lord's Day takes on its full meaning. It is then that man enters the depths of God's "rest" and can experience a tremor of the Creator's joy when, after the creation, He saw that all He had made "was very good" (Genesis 1:31).

The First Day of the Week

According to the common witness of the Gospels, the Resurrection of Jesus Christ from the dead took place on "the first day after the Sabbath" (Mark 16:2,9; Luke 24:1; John 20:1). On the same day, the Risen Lord appeared to the two disciples of

Emmaus (Luke 24:13-35) and to the eleven Apostles gathered together (Luke 24:36; John 20:19). A week later, as the Gospel of John recounts (20:26), the disciples were gathered together once again, when Jesus appeared to them and made himself known to Thomas by showing him the signs of his Passion. The day of Pentecost, the first day of the eighth week after the Jewish Passover (Acts 2:1), when the promise made by Jesus to the Apostles after the Resurrection was fulfilled by the outpouring of the Holy Spirit (Luke 24:49; Acts 1:4-5) also fell on a Sunday. This was the day of the first proclamation and the first baptisms: Peter announced to the assembled crowd that Christ was risen and *"those who received his word were baptized" (Acts 2:41)*. This was the epiphany of the Church, revealed as the people into which are gathered in unity, beyond all their differences, the scattered children of God.

It was for this reason that, from Apostolic times, "the first day after the Sabbath," the first day of the week, began to shape the rhythm of life for Christ's disciples (1 Corinthians 16:2). The first day after the Sabbath was also the day upon which the faithful of Troas were gathered for the breaking of bread, when Paul bade them farewell and miraculously restored the young Eutychus to life (Acts 20:7-12). The Book of Revelation gives evidence of the practice of calling the first day of the week "the Lord's Day" (1:10). This would now be a characteristic distinguishing Christians from the world around them. As early as the beginning of the second century, it was noted by Pliny the Younger, governor of Bithynia, in his report on the Christian practice "of gathering together on a set day before sunrise and singing among themselves a hymn to Christ as to a god"(9). And when Christians spoke of the "Lord's Day", they did so giving to this term the full sense of the Easter proclamation: "Jesus Christ is Lord" (Philippians 2:11; Acts 2:36; 1 Corinthians 12:3). Thus Christ was given the same title which the Septuagint used to translate what in the revelation of the Old Testament was the unutterable name of God: YHWH.

Growing Distinction from the Sabbath
It was this newness which the catechesis of the first centuries stressed as it sought to show the prominence of Sunday relative to the Jewish Sabbath. It was on the Sabbath that the Jewish people had to gather in the synagogue and to rest in the way prescribed by the Law. The Apostles, and in particular Paul, continued initially to attend the synagogue so that there they might proclaim Jesus Christ, commenting upon *"the words of the prophets which are read every Sabbath" (Acts 13:27)*. Some communities observed the Sabbath while also celebrating Sunday. Soon, however, the two days began to be distinguished ever more clearly, in reaction chiefly to the insistence of those Christians whose origins in Judaism made them inclined to maintain the obligation of the old Law (10). Saint Augustine notes: "Therefore the Lord too has placed his seal on his day, which is the third after the Passion. In the weekly cycle, however, it is the eighth day after the seventh, that is after the Sabbath, and the first day of the week"(11).

The Day of the New Creation
A comparison of the Christian Sunday with the Old Testament vision of the Sabbath prompted the unique connection between the Resurrection and Creation. Christian thought spontaneously linked the Resurrection, which took place on "the first day of the week", with the first day of that cosmic week (Genesis 1:1 - 2:4) which shapes the creation story in the Book of Genesis: the day of the creation of light (1:3-5). This

link invited an understanding of the Resurrection as the beginning of a new creation, the first fruits of which is the glorious Christ, *"the first born of all creation" (Colossians 1:15)* and "the first born from the dead" (1:18).

The Day of the Gift of the Spirit

Sunday, the day of light, could also be called the day of "fire", in reference to the Holy Spirit. The light of Christ is intimately linked to the "fire" of the Spirit, and the two images together reveal the meaning of the Christian Sunday (12). When he appeared to the Apostles on the evening of Easter, Jesus breathed upon them and said: *Receive the Holy Spirit. If you forgive the sins of any, they are forgiven; if you retain the sins of any, they are retained (John 20:22-23).* The outpouring of the Spirit was the great gift of the Risen Lord to his disciples on Easter Sunday. It was again Sunday when, fifty days after the Resurrection, the Spirit descended in power, as *"a mighty wind"* and *"fire" (Acts 2:2-3),* upon the Apostles gathered with Mary. Pentecost is not only the founding event of the Church, but is also the mystery which forever gives life to the Church. The "weekly Easter" thus becomes additionally, in a sense, the "weekly Pentecost," when Christians relive the Apostles' joyful encounter with the Risen Lord and receive the life-giving breath of His Spirit.

The Day of Faith

Given these different dimensions that set it apart, Sunday appears as the supreme day of faith. It is the day when, by the power of the Holy Spirit, who is the Church's living "memory" (John. 14:26), the first appearance of the Risen Lord becomes an event renewed in the "today" of each of Christ's disciples. Gathered in his presence in the Sunday assembly, believers sense themselves called like the Apostle Thomas: *"Put your finger here, and see my hands. Put out your hand, and place it in my side. Doubt no longer, but believe" (John 20:27).* Yes, Sunday is the day of faith. Listening to the word and receiving the Body of the Lord, the baptized contemplate the Risen Jesus present in the "holy signs" and confess with the Apostle Thomas: *"My Lord and my God!" (John 20:28).*

The Fulfillment of the Sabbath

This aspect of the Christian Sunday shows in a special way how it is the fulfillment of the Old Testament Sabbath. On the Lord's Day, which, as we have already said, the Old Testament links to the work of creation (Genesis 2:1-3; Exodus 20:8-11) and the Exodus (Deuteronomy. 5:12-15), the Christian is called to proclaim the new creation and the new covenant brought about in the Mystery of Christ. Far from being abolished, the celebration of creation becomes more profound within a Christocentric perspective, being seen in the light of God's plan *"to unite all things in Christ, things in heaven and things on earth" (Ephesians 1:10).* The remembrance of the liberation of the Exodus also assumes its full meaning, as it becomes a remembrance of the universal redemption accomplished by Christ in his Death and Resurrection. More than a "replacement" for the Sabbath, therefore, *Sunday is its fulfillment*, and in a certain sense its extension and full expression in the ordered unfolding of the history of salvation, which reaches its culmination in Christ.

In this perspective, the biblical theology of the "Sabbath" can be recovered in full, without compromising the Christian character of Sunday. It is a theology that leads us ever anew and in unfailing awe to the mystery of the beginning, when the eternal Word of God, by a free decision of love, created the world from nothing. The work of creation was sealed by the blessing and consecration of the day on which God ceased *"from all the work which he had done in creation" (Genesis 2:3).*

It is the duty of Christians therefore to remember that, although the practices of the Jewish Sabbath are gone, surpassed as they are by the fulfillment which Sunday brings, the underlying reasons for keeping the Lord's Day holy, inscribed solemnly in the Ten Commandments, remain valid, though they need to be reinterpreted in the light of the theology and spirituality of Sunday: (Deuteronomy 5:12-15).

Christ came to accomplish a new exodus, to restore freedom to the oppressed. He performed many healings on the Sabbath (Matthew 12:9-14 and parallels), certainly not to violate the Lord's Day, but to reveal its full meaning: *"The Sabbath was made for man, not man for the Sabbath" (Mark 2:27).* Opposing the excessively legalistic interpretation of some of his contemporaries, and developing the true meaning of the biblical Sabbath, Jesus, as "Lord of the Sabbath" (Mark 2:28), restores to the Sabbath observance its liberating character, carefully safeguarding the rights of God and the rights of man.

The Second Coming of Christ

Since Sunday is the weekly Easter, recalling and making present the day upon which Christ rose from the dead, it is also the day that reveals the meaning of time. It has nothing in common with the cosmic cycles according to which natural religion and human culture tend to impose a structure on time, succumbing perhaps to the myth of eternal return. The Christian Sunday is wholly other! Springing from the Resurrection, it cuts through human time, the months, the years, the centuries, like a directional arrow which points them towards their target: Christ's Second Coming. Sunday foreshadows the last day, which in a way is already anticipated by Christ's glory in the event of the Resurrection.

In fact, everything that will happen until the end of the world will be no more than an extension and unfolding of what happened on the day when the battered body of the Crucified Lord was raised by the power of the Spirit and became in turn the wellspring of the Spirit for all humanity. Christians know that there is no need to wait for another time of salvation, since, however long the world may last, they are already living in *the last times*. Not only the Church, but the cosmos itself and history are ceaselessly ruled and governed by the glorified Christ. It is this life force which propels creation, *"groaning in birth-pangs until now" (Romans 8:22)*, towards the goal of its full redemption. Mankind can have only a faint intuition of this process, but Christians have the key and the certainty. Keeping Sunday holy is the important witness that they are called to bear, so that every stage of human history will be upheld by hope.

Footnotes for Chapter One

1- Marguerite Ickis. *The Book of Religious Holidays and Celebrations.* p. 5. *(and of course the Bible in Exodus 20:8)*

2- http://www.jewfaq.org/shabbat.htm

3- Barney Kasdan. *God's Appointed Times*. p. 2.

4- Samuele Bacchiocchi. *From Sabbath To Sunday*. p. 9.

5- *Mishnah* Shabbat, 7:2

6- 2- http://www.jewfaq.org/shabbat.htm

7- *The Didaché* 14, 1, Saint Ignatius of Antioch, *To the Magnesians* 9, 1-2; SC 10, 88-89.

8- St Gregory. *Epistle*. 13,1.

9- Pliny the Younger. *Epistle*. 10, 96, 7. Tertullian *Apologeticum* 2, 6.

10- Victor Buksbazen. *The Gospel in the Feasts of Israel*. p. 75.

11- Augustine. *Sermon 8 in the Octave of Easter* 4: PL 46, 841.

12- Clement of Alexandria, *Stromata*, VI, 138, 1-2: *PG* 9, 364.

Chapter Two – Purim
February/March (Adar)

In the twelfth month, which is the month of Adar, on its thirteenth day... on the day that the enemies of the Jews were expected to prevail over them, it was turned about: the Jews prevailed over their adversaries. - Esther 9:1

And they gained relief on the fourteenth, making it a day of feasting and gladness. - Esther 9:17

[Mordecai instructed them] to observe them as days of feasting and gladness, and sending delicacies to one another, and gifts to the poor. - Esther 9:22

What is Purim?

Purim (from Akkadian pūru) is one of the most joyous and fun holidays on the Jewish calendar. It commemorates a time when the Jewish people living in Persia (about 450 BC) were saved from extermination by Haman's plot to annihilate all the Jews of the Persian Empire, who had survived the Babylonian captivity, after Persia had conquered Babylonia who in turn had destroyed the First Temple and dispersed the Jewish people. This feast is named after the "lot" which Haman cast in order to pick the day on which to destroy the Jews. On that chosen day, however, the Jews were victoriously saved and Mordicai suggested that this be a day that Jews commemorate for all times (Esther 9:17-24) (1).

The story of Purim is told in the book of Esther. The heroes of the story are Esther, a beautiful young Jewish woman living in Persia, and her cousin Mordecai, who raised her as if she were his daughter. Esther was taken to the house of Ahasuerus, King of Persia, to become part of his harem. King Ahasuerus loved Esther more than his other women and made Esther queen, but the King did not know that Esther was a Jew, because Mordecai told her not to reveal her identity.

The villain of the story is Haman, an arrogant, egotistical advisor to the King. Haman hated Mordecai because Mordecai refused to bow down to Haman, so Haman plotted to destroy the Jewish people. In a speech that is all too familiar to Jews, Haman told the king, "*There is a certain people scattered abroad and dispersed among the peoples in all the provinces of your realm. Their laws are different from those of every other people's, and they do not observe the King's laws; therefore it is not befitting the King to tolerate them*" (Esther 3:8). The King gave the fate of the Jewish people to Haman, to do as he pleased to them. Haman planned to exterminate all of the Jews and picked the day to destroy them by casting lots.

Mordecai persuaded Esther to speak to the King on behalf of the Jewish people. This was a dangerous thing for Esther to do, because anyone who came into the King's presence without being summoned could be put to death, and she had not been summoned. Esther fasted for three days to prepare herself, and then went into the King. He welcomed her. Later, she told him of Haman's plot against her people. The Jewish people were saved, and Haman was hanged on the gallows that had been prepared for

Mordecai.

The book of Esther is unusual in that it is the only book of the Bible that does not contain the name of God. Mordecai makes a vague reference to the fact that the Jews will be saved by someone else, if not by Esther, but that is as close as the book comes to mentioning God. The Book records a series of apparently unrelated events which took place over a nine-year period during the reign of King Ahasuerus. These events, when seen as a whole, depict the "coincidences" as evidence of Divine intervention operating behind the scenes, according to interpretations by Talmudic and other major commentaries on the Megillah (scroll of Esther). The main lesson of the book is God's faithfulness to His covenant people - *I will bless those who bless you, and whoever curses you I will curse; and all peoples on earth will be blessed through you." (Genesis 12:3).*

When is Purim?

Purim is the last Biblical Feast of the year and is celebrated on the 14th day of Adar, which is usually in March and is exactly one month before Passover (2) (See Appendix 2). The 13th of Adar is the day that Haman chose for the extermination of the Jews, and the day that the Jews battled their enemies for their lives. On the day afterwards, the 14th, they celebrated their survival. In cities that were walled in the time of Joshua, Purim is celebrated on the 15th of the month, because the book of Esther says that in Shushan (a walled city), deliverance from the massacre was not complete until the next day. The 15th is referred to as Shushan Purim (3).

In leap years, when there are two months of Adar, Purim is celebrated in the second month of Adar, so it is always one month before Passover. The 14th day of the first Adar in a leap year is celebrated as a minor holiday called Purim Katan, which means "little Purim." There are no specific observances for Purim Katan; however, a person should celebrate the holiday and should not mourn or fast. Some communities also observe a Purim Katan on the anniversary of any day when their community was saved from a catastrophe, destruction, evil or oppression.

What are the Purim Customs?

The Purim holiday is preceded by a minor fast, on the 13th of Adar called the Fast of Esther, which commemorates Esther's three days of fasting in preparation for her meeting with the King (Esther 4:16). If Purim falls on a Sunday, the fast day is observed on the preceding Thursday instead of on the preceding day which would be the Sabbath. Unlike the fast of Yom Kippur, the Day of Atonement, which is observed from sunset to sunset, the fast of Esther begins with daybreak and lasts till sunset, during which time food and drink of any kind are forbidden, but not such physical conveniences as bathing.

On Purim a special prayer ("*Al ha-Nissim*"—"For the Miracles") is inserted into the Shemoneh Esrei ("The Eighteen Blessings" the central prayer of the Jewish liturgy). It is also included during evening, morning and afternoon prayers, as well as is included in the grace after Meals.

Because the holiday of Purim has been held in high esteem by Judaism at all times; some have held that when all the prophetical works are forgotten, the Book of

Esther will still be remembered, and, accordingly, the Feast of Purim will continue to be observed (4). Like Chanukkah, Purim's status as a holiday is on a lesser level than those days ordained holy by the Torah. Purim is not subject to the Sabbath-like restrictions on work that some other holidays have; however, some sources indicate that we should not go about our ordinary business on Purim out of respect for the holiday. Accordingly, business transactions and even manual labor are allowed on Purim.

However, the primary commandment related to Purim is to hear the reading of the book of Esther a regulation ascribed in the Talmud, to the "Sages of the Great Assembly" (an assembly of 72 Rabbis in the period after the time of the prophets up to the time of the development of Rabbinic Judaism), of which Mordechai is reported to have been a member (5). The book of Esther is commonly known as the Megillah, as mentioned earlier. Although there are five books of Jewish scripture that are properly referred to as "megillahs" (Esther, Ruth, Ecclesiastes, Song of Songs, and Lamentations), this is the one people usually mean when they speak of "The" Megillah. Originally this enactment was for the 14th of Adar only; later, however, Rabbis prescribed that the Megillah should also be read on the eve of Purim.

Rabbis also obliged women to attend the reading of the Megillah, inasmuch as it was a woman, Queen Esther, through whom the miraculous deliverance of the Jews was accomplished. Women have an obligation to hear the megilla because "they also were involved in that miracle." Most Orthodox communities, including Modern Orthodox ones, however, generally do not allow women to lead the megilla reading except in rare circumstances. Authorities who hold that women should not read the megilla for themselves, because of a question as to which blessing they should recite upon the reading, nonetheless agree that they have an obligation to hear it read. According to these authorities if women, or men for that matter, cannot attend the services in the synagogue, the megilla should be read for them in private by any male over the age of thirteen. Often in Orthodox communities there is a special public reading only for women, conducted either in a private home or in a synagogue, but the Megillah is read by a man. Some Orthodox authorities have held that women can serve as public Megillah readers. Women's megilla readings have become increasingly common in more liberal Modern Orthodox Judaism, however they may only read for other women.

According to the Mishnah, Exodus 17:8-16, the story of the attack on the Jews by Amalek, the ancestor of Haman, is also to be read. In Esther 3:1 Haman, is called the Agagite, which is interpreted as being a descendant of the Amalekite King Agag. So in Jewish tradition, the Amalekites came to represent the archetypal enemy of the Jews.

Purim is an occasion on which much joyous license is permitted within the walls of the synagogue itself. It is customary that, while The Megillah is being read, people are to boo, hiss, stamp feet and rattle gragers (noisemakers) whenever the name of Haman is mentioned. The purpose of this custom is to "blot out the name of Haman" (6). Haman is mentioned 54 times so there would be a great deal of commotion going on during this reading! This is done in accordance with a passage in the Midrash, where the verse "Thou shalt blot out the remembrance of Amalek" (Deuteronomy 25:19) is explained to mean "even from wood and stones", the rabbis introduced the custom of writing the name of Haman, the offspring of Amalek, on two smooth stones and of knocking or rubbing them constantly until the name was blotted out.

Ultimately, the stones fell into disuse, with the knocking alone remaining. Some wrote the name of Haman on the soles of their shoes, and at the mention of the name stamped with their feet as a sign of contempt. For noisemaking, others used a noisy rattle, called in Hebrew a *ra'ashan* ("noise") and in Yiddish a *gragger/gregga*. Some of the Rabbis protested against these uproarious excesses, considering them a disturbance of public worship, but the custom of using noisemakers in synagogue on Purim is now almost universal.

On this feast day we are also commanded to eat, drink and be merry during Purim. Esther and Mordecai proclaimed that Purim was to be a time of feasting and merrymaking (Esther 9:17, 22). This ordinance developed into the special Purim meal, which takes place during daylight hours on the holiday. The Jews believe that it is a most appropriate way to commemorate their success against a decree meant to physically destroy them, since it gives pleasure to the body. As a secular meal, it does not include a blessing over the wine, but nonetheless encourages partaking of plenty of wine. In fact, the most notable feature of the Purim meal is the injunction, uncharacteristic among Jews, to drink.

This is not an invitation to drink uncontrollably, but a way to recognize your limit. Once you reach the point of confusion, stop. (You are responsible for any damage caused by merrymaking and intoxication!) You are not supposed to get rip-roaring drunk on Purim, but happily tipsy. Not only does wine add to frivolity, it highlights the theme of drinking and how it helped create the miracle, throughout the Purim story. The saga opens with a series of wine-infused banquets (Esther 1:1-9), Esther's coronation is celebrated with a banquet (2:18), the Jews' fate is sealed with a banquet between Ahasuerus and Haman (3:15), Esther hosts two banquets for the King and Haman (5:6, 6:7), and the book ends with the Jews celebrating and agreeing to annually celebrate with feasts (9:17-19).

According to the Talmud, a person is required to drink until he cannot tell the difference between "cursed be Haman" and "blessed be Mordecai," though opinions differ as to exactly how drunk that is. A person certainly should not become so drunk that he might violate other commandments or get seriously ill. In addition, recovering alcoholics or others who might suffer serious harm from alcohol are exempt from this obligation.

It is also customary to hold carnival-like celebrations on Purim, to perform plays and parodies, and to hold beauty contests. Americans sometimes refer to Purim as the Jewish Mardi Gras.

Purim is a time for other unusual goings-on as well. For example, many congregations will read the prayers in ways that would be considered sacrilegious on any other occasion during the year—for example, singing some prayers to the tune of widely-known songs, to add to the levity—or employing melodies used on other Jewish holidays. Additionally, many people dress up in costumes. There will be many Esthers, Mordechais and even a few Hamans in the synagogue on the festival (7).

17

Outside the synagogue, pranks have been carried even to a greater extreme. Some of them date from the Talmudic period. As early as the fifth century, and especially in the 9th and 10th centuries, it was a custom to burn Haman in effigy on Purim. However, this burning custom, which persisted into the 20th century, is no longer practiced. These customs often aroused the wrath of Christians, who interpreted them as a disguised attempt to ridicule Jesus and the Cross.

In addition, the Rabbis commanded the people to send out gifts of food or drink, and to make gifts to charity based on what Esther did. The Book of Esther prescribes "the sending of portions one man to another, and gifts to the poor" (9:22). Over time, this commandment has become one of the most prominent features of the celebration of Purim. According to Jewish Religious Law, each Jew over the age of 12 (girls) or 13 (boys) must send two different, ready made foods to one friend, and two charitable donations (either money or food) to two poor people. The gifts to friends are called the "sending of portions", and often include wine and pastries; alternately, sweets, snacks, salads or any foodstuff qualifies. Synagogues and schools often run a collective Purim Project that manages the "sending of portions" or *Mishloach Manot Baskets* to all members. These projects are typically one of the best annual fundraisers in many synagogues and schools.

Although the sending of *mishloach manot* is technically limited to two gifts for one friend, for some the custom has evolved into a major gift-giving event. Families often prepare dozens of homemade and store-bought food baskets to deliver to friends, neighbors, and relatives on Purim day.

In the synagogue, regular collections of charity are made on the festival and the money is distributed among the needy. No distinction was to be made among the poor; anyone who was willing to accept charity is allowed to participate. It is obligatory upon the poorest Jew, even one who is himself dependent on charity, to give to other poor people.

Other Purim Celebrations

In addition to the official Purim, other occasions arose to celebrate deliverance of communities or families from the threat of annihilation. These celebrations were also called Purims. Until recently, many Jewish communities around the world celebrated local "Purims" that commemorated its deliverance from a particular anti-semitic ruler or group. The best known is *Purim Vintz*, traditionally celebrated in Frankfurt am Main, one week after the regular Purim. This commemorates the Fettmilch uprising (1616-1620), in which one Vincenz Fettmilch attempted to exterminate the Jewish community in Frankfurt but failed.

Many Jewish families have also had "family Purims" throughout the centuries, celebrated at home, whereby they celebrate their escape from persecution, an accident, or any other type of misfortune. For example, in Krakow, Poland, Rabbi Yom Tov Lipmann Heller (1579-1654) asked that his family henceforth celebrate a private Purim, marking the end of his many troubles, including having faced trumped-up charges.

Jesus and Purim

Although the name of God does not appear anywhere in the Book of Esther, we see His sovereign presence throughout. The celebration of Purim is a joyous remembrance of God's deliverance of His people through an attempted annihilation. This fact is especially significant in light of the fact that these events took place before the incarnation of Messiah Jesus. Therefore, Purim stands as another reminder that God keeps His promises; He preserved and protected the vehicle (the Jewish people) through which Messiah would come just as He said He would and showed that attempts to eliminate His Chosen People are futile.

Purim is a scriptural holiday that the Jews were commanded to celebrate in the book of Esther, but there is no specific tie to Jesus in Purim as there are in the other holidays. It is possible that Jesus celebrated the feast of Purim in John 5. In this chapter the Lord Jesus is up in Jerusalem for an unnamed feast. Scholars have debated whether the feast was Passover, Purim, Succoth or even Pentecost. Some have objected to Purim because it is a "minor" feast and not one of the three "major" pilgrimage festivals (Deut. 16:16). That argument is irrelevant because Jesus also celebrated another "minor" holiday, Hanukkah (John 10:22). Chronologically, the only feast that makes sense is Purim in AD 28. The feast of John 5 fell on a Sabbath (5:9). Scholars such as Faulstich say that the only feast day to fall on a Sabbath between AD 25 and AD 35 was Purim of AD 28 (8).

To expand on this a bit, if Jesus did celebrate Purim then He took full advantage of the Feast to teach His disciples about Himself and to fulfill the commandment to give gifts to the poor. John tells us that by the Sheep Pool is a another pool called the Pool of Bethesda. The word "Bethesda" is made up of two Hebrew words, "beit" and "hesed", meaning "house of mercy." At this pool there was a sick man who had been lying on his bed for thirty-eight years. The Lord Jesus approached him to offer him a Purim gift, i.e. good health. He said, "Do you want to be made well" (John 5:6)? The man responded in the affirmative but he added that he had nobody to place him into the pool when the water was stirred up (5:7). The Lord Jesus said to him, "Rise, take up your bed and walk" (5:8). The man accepted the gift and he was healed instantly.

This was also the first time in His public ministry that Jesus declared that "God was His Father, making Himself equal with God" (5:18). He also said that He was the "Son of God" (5:25) and the "Son of Man" (5:27).

Purim was one of many episodes in God's dealings with His people. The Jews were saved physically at this point in their history. The time of their full salvation and the complete fulfillment of God's prophecies given to Abraham were drawing nigh. It happened five hundred years later with the coming of the Lord Jesus, the Messiah. He was the greater Mordecai. Condemned to die for His people, Jesus the Messiah became the supreme sacrifice of atonement for the sins of Jew and Gentile alike. In Him were truly fulfilled the prophecies of old, *"...All the nations of the earth shall be blessed in him" (Genesis 18:18).*

Mordecai and Esther knew for certain that Haman's decree was not an accident of history, but a consequence of failings within the Jewish people. That is why Mordecai's response was *"He clothed himself in sackcloth and ashes and went out into the midst of the City."* He turned to repentance, and urged the rest of the Jews to do likewise. Only then did he send Esther *"to come to the King and entreat him and plead with him for her people."* Esther was also repentant. She asked Mordecai to *"Go and gather all the Jews ... and they should fast for me, and neither eat nor drink for three days and nights." In addition, Esther included herself: "I also...will fast likewise."* Just as the Jews were rescued, so our Righteous Messiah redeems us.

Though Purim is not specifically mentioned in the New Covenant, the themes involved are of considerable importance to believers in Jesus as Messiah. The providential hand of God is a major theme in Esther. Time and time again in the Scriptures that which man meant for evil God used for the salvation of His people. Psalm 22 occupies a central place in the Jewish celebration. This is, of course, the Psalm Jesus quoted from the cross. *"My God, My God, Why have you forsaken me?"* Haman sought the destruction of the people of God, yet the Sovereign God not only preserved His covenant people but also judged those who opposed Him. Many saw and feared and turned to the Living LORD of Israel. Ironically, if it wasn't for the impalement (a form of crucifixion) of Haman and the deliverance of the Jewish people, the Messiah couldn't have come to deliver both Jews and Gentiles by hanging on a tree himself. Wicked men, both Roman and Jewish leaders, delivered him to death but God intended it for our deliverance.

Conclusion

It is interesting that even though this holiday is one of the most fun and exciting holidays of the Jews, at the same time, most Jewish scholars today believe that the book of Esther is essentially a work of fiction and that the events in it never happened. The view is that the Jews, who were slaves, servants and a minority among the Persians, simply adopted Persian New Year traditions and customs changing them to fit the Jewish culture (9). One example of the Jewish changes is the very names of Esther and Mordecai, which, according to the scholars, were changed from Ishtar and Marduk (10).

For those of us who believe in the inerrancy and authority of Scripture we know the account of Esther to be true. We rejoice in the salvation of God's people and the prophetic backdrop it is to the saving work of Jesus Christ in our hearts and lives today. How faithful the Lord is to all of us at all times.

Some Interesting Symbolism

1.) The picture of the three day death and resurrection of Jesus is shown. Esther fasted for three days, and then on the third day she arose to go before the King and begin the work of saving her people from the evil plans and schemes of Haman.

2.) The story of Esther is a depiction of a Christian's walk in a new life. Exposing Haman is symbolic of exposing sin. The new decree triumphs. The old decree symbolizes Jesus triumphing over the law of sin and death. Once Haman (sin, flesh) was put to death, Mordecai (Holy Spirit) is given unlimited command and we are given new life.

3.) The text of Esther says that Haman was hung. Interestingly to be "hung" in

Persia was not to be hung by rope on a gallows such as modern time executions. Rather this kind of hanging meant to be impaled or nailed to a post in a version of crucifixion. These posts were ready for the people of God to be hung on by Haman. But the people were delivered from the hanging by God's intervention. So also Jesus delivers His people from death by being "hung" on the cross in our place.

Footnotes for Chapter Two

1- Alfred Edershiem. *The Temple.* p. 214.

2- Kevin Howard. The Feasts of the Lord. p. 178.

3- Arlene Cardozo. *Jewish Family Celebrations.* p. 105.

4- Jerusalem Talmud, *Megillah 1/5a*; Maimonides, *Yad*, Megilla.

5- Jerusalem Talmud, *Megilla 2*.

6- Judaism 101. www.jewfaq.org/holiday9.htm.

7-Barney Kasdan. *God's Appointed Times.* p. 128.

8- Faulstich, E. W. *1986 Computer Calendar: IBM Software.*

9- Philip Goodman. *The Purim Anthology.* p. 6.

10- Michael Strassfeld. *The Jewish Holidays, A Guide & Commentary.* p. 188.

Chapter Three – Easter
March/April

13If there is no resurrection of the dead, then not even Christ has been raised. 14And if Christ has not been raised, our preaching is useless and so is your faith. 17And if Christ has not been raised, your faith is futile; you are still in your sins. 18Then those also who have fallen asleep in Christ are lost. 19If only for this life we have hope in Christ, we are to be pitied more than all men. (I Cor. 15:13-14, 17-19)

~~~~~~~~~~~~~~~~~~~~~~~~~~~~~~~~~~~~`

5The angel said to the women, "Do not be afraid, for I know that you are looking for Jesus, who was crucified. 6He is not here; he has risen, just as he said. Come and see the place where he lay. 9Suddenly Jesus met them. "Greetings," he said. They came to him, clasped his feet and worshiped him. 10Then Jesus said to them "Do not be afraid. Go and tell my brothers to go to Galilee; there they will see me." (Matthew 28:5-6, 9-10)

5As they entered the tomb, they saw a young man dressed in a white robe sitting on the right side, and they were alarmed. 6"Don't be alarmed," he said. "You are looking for Jesus the Nazarene, who was crucified. He has risen! He is not here. See the place where they laid him. (Mark 16:5-6)

5In their fright the women bowed down with their faces to the ground, but the men said to them, "Why do you look for the living among the dead? 6He is not here; he has risen! Remember how he told you, while he was still with you in Galilee: 7'The Son of Man must be delivered into the hands of sinful men, be crucified and on the third day be raised again.'" 8Then they remembered his words. (Luke 24:5-8)

6Then Simon Peter, who was behind him, arrived and went into the tomb. He saw the strips of linen lying there, 7as well as the burial cloth that had been around Jesus' head. The cloth was folded up by itself, separate from the linen. 11Mary stood outside the tomb crying. As she wept, she bent over to look into the tomb 12and saw two angels in white, seated where Jesus' body had been, one at the head and the other at the foot. 13They asked her, "Woman, why are you crying?" "They have taken my Lord away," she said, "and I don't know where they have put him." 14At this, she turned around and saw Jesus standing there, but she did not realize that it was Jesus. 15"Woman," he said, "Why are you crying? Who is it you are looking for?" Thinking he was the gardener, she said, "Sir, if you have carried him away, tell me where you have put him, and I will get him." 16Jesus said to her, "Mary." She turned toward him and cried out in Aramaic, "Rabboni!" (which means Teacher).

17Jesus said, "Do not hold on to me, for I have not yet returned to the Father. Go instead to my brothers and tell them, 'I am returning to my Father and your Father, to my God and your God.'" 18Mary Magdalene went to the disciples with the news: "I have seen the Lord!" And she told them that he had said these things to her. (John 20:1-18)

The Events of Easter Sunday
Here is an outline of a *possible harmony* of the Evangelists' account concerning

the principal events of Easter Sunday:

The women carrying the spices previously prepared start out for the sepulcher before dawn, and reach it after sunrise; they are anxious about the heavy stone, but know nothing of the official guard of the sepulcher (Matthew 28:1-3; Mark 16:1-3; Luke 24:1; John 20:1).

The angel frightened the guards by his brightness, put them to flight, rolled away the stone, and seated himself not upon (*ep autou*), but above (*epano autou*) the stone (Matthew 28:2-4).

Mary Magdalene and Mary the Mother of James, and Salome and another woman approach the sepulcher, and see the stone rolled back, whereupon Mary Magdalene immediately returns to inform the Apostles (Mark 16:4; Luke 24:2; John 20:1-2).

The other two women enter the sepulcher, find an angel seated in the vestibule, who shows them the empty sepulcher, announces the Resurrection, and commissions them to tell the disciples and Peter that they shall see Jesus in Galilee (Matthew 28:5-7; Mark 16:5-7).

A second group of women, consisting of Joanna and her companions, arrive at the sepulcher, where they have probably agreed to meet the first group, enter the empty interior, and are admonished by two angels that Jesus has risen according to His prediction (Luke 24:10).

Not long after, Peter and John, who were notified by Mary Magdalene, arrive at the sepulcher and find the linen cloth in such a position as to exclude the supposition that the body was stolen; for they lay simply flat on the ground, showing that the sacred body had vanished out of them without touching them. When John notices this he believes (John 20:3-10).

Mary Magdalene returns to the sepulcher, sees first two angels within, and then Jesus Himself (John 20:11-16; Mark 16:9).

The two groups of women, who probably met on their return to the city, are favored with the sight of Christ arisen, who commissions them to tell His brethren that they will see him in Galilee (Matthew 28:8-10; Mark 16:8).

The women relate their experiences to the Apostles, but find no belief (Mark 16:10-11; Luke 24:9-11).

Jesus appears to the disciples, at Emmaus, and they return to Jerusalem; the Apostles appear to waver between doubt and belief (Mark 16:12-13; Luke 24:13-35). Christ appears to Peter, and therefore Peter and John firmly believe in the Resurrection (Luke 24:34; John 20:8).

After the return of the disciples from Emmaus, Jesus appears to all the Apostles excepting Thomas (Mark 16:14; Luke 24:36-43; John 20:19-25). The harmony of the other apparitions of Christ after His Resurrection presents no special difficulties.

Briefly, therefore, the fact of Christ's Resurrection is attested by more than 500 eyewitnesses, whose experience, simplicity, and uprightness of life rendered them incapable of inventing such a fable, who lived at a time when any attempt to deceive could have been easily discovered, who had nothing in this life to gain, but everything to lose by their testimony, whose moral courage exhibited in their apostolic life can be explained only by their intimate conviction of the objective truth of their message.

Again the fact of Christ's Resurrection is attested by the eloquent silence of the Synagogue which had done everything to prevent deception, which could have easily discovered deception, if there had been any, which opposed only sleeping witnesses to the testimony of the Apostles, which did not punish the alleged carelessness of the official guard, and which could not answer the testimony of the Apostles except by threatening them "that they speak no more in this name to any man" (Acts 4:17). Finally the thousands and millions, both Jews and Gentiles, who believed the testimony of the Apostles in spite of all the disadvantages following from such a belief, in short the origin of the Church, requires for its explanation the reality of Christ's Resurrection, for the rise of the Church without the Resurrection would have been a greater miracle than the Resurrection itself.

What is Easter?

As we have just seen from the Scriptures, Easter is the celebration of the resurrection of Jesus Christ from the dead. What do we mean by the resurrection of Christ? Jesus Christ came into this world to die as our substitute for our sins. The sinless Son of God came to give His life as a ransom for many (Matt. 20:28). On that first Good Friday, Jesus was crucified. We know He died because one of the Roman soldiers pierced Jesus' side with a spear to ensure His death. Some of his disciples then buried His body in a new tomb (John 19:30-42).

On the third day Jesus was raised from the dead with a transformed body that was clothed with immortality and glory. His resurrection body could appear and disappear, go through material objects, and ascend to and descend from heaven. The Resurrection is the foretaste of the consummation of all things. The promise of Advent is fulfilled in Easter (1).

Easter is the fundamental and most important celebration of the Christian Faith and of the Church. Every other religious festival on our calendars, including Christmas, is secondary in importance to the celebration of the Resurrection of Jesus Christ. This is very clearly reflected in the customs of the cultures of countries that traditionally have Christian majorities. Commemorating the slaying of the true Lamb of God and the Resurrection of Christ, the cornerstone upon which the Christian faith is built, is the oldest feast and celebration of the Christian Church. The Resurrection of Jesus is the connecting link between the Old and New Testaments and the basis of our eternal future.

The connection between the Jewish Passover and the Christian feast of Easter is real and ideal. Real, since Christ died on the Feast of Passover; ideal, like the relation between type and reality, because Christ's death and resurrection had its figures and types in the Old Law, particularly in the paschal lamb, which was eaten towards evening of the 14th of Nisan. In fact, the Jewish feast was taken over into the Christian Easter celebration; the liturgy sings of the passing of Israel through the Red Sea, the paschal lamb, the column of fire, etc. Apart, however, from the Jewish feast, the Christians would have still celebrated the anniversary of the death and the resurrection of Christ, as the Apostles and early Christians did.

This is not to say that Christmas and other elements of the Christian calendar are ignored. Instead, these events are all seen as necessary but *preliminary* to the full climax of the Resurrection, in which all that has come before reaches fulfillment and fruition. Easter is the primary act that fulfills the purpose of Christ's ministry on earth—to defeat death by dying and to purify and exalt humanity by voluntarily assuming and overcoming human frailty.

The Name of the Holiday

"Easter" is the name of the day on which we celebrate the Resurrection of Jesus Christ. It also refers to the season of the church year, called Eastertide or the Easter Season. Traditionally the Easter Season lasted for the forty days from Easter Day until Ascension Day but now officially lasts for the fifty days until Pentecost. The first week of the Easter Season is known as Easter Week.

This length of the Easter season holiday is based upon the Jewish festival of "Shavuot" (Hebrew for "Weeks") and the counting of the "Omer" (a measurement – in this case meaning "Days"). This begins immediately after the start of Passover. Each day is counted and after 7 weeks have past (49 days) the important holiday of Shavuot (Pentecost) is celebrated on the 50th day. Early Jewish Christians apparently included this ritual in Christianity, hence the counting of 49+1 day from Easter, which was originally counted according to the Jewish date for the Feast of First Fruits, 16th of Nissan, to Pentecost.

In most languages of Christian societies the holiday's name is derived from *Pesach*, the Hebrew name for Passover, but not all of them. The English name, "Easter", and the German, "Ostern," derive from the name of an Anglo-Saxon Goddess of the Dawn (thus, of spring, as the dawn of the year) — called Ēaster, Ēastre, and Ēostre in various dialects of Old English. In England, the annual festive time in her honor was in the "Month of Easter" or Ēostur-monath, equivalent to April/Aprilis. The Venerable Bede wrote in the 8th century: "Eostur-month, which is now interpreted as the paschal month, was formerly named after the goddess Eostre, and has given its name to the festival" (2).

It is interesting to note that Bede's reference to Eostre is the only reference known of this goddess and yet the world has made this a major point of attack against the Christian roots of the celebration of Easter. Some would argue that Eostre is suspiciously like Ashteroth and Ishtar. However, none of them have anything to do with Easter, or the name Easter, which is uniquely Teutonic. Lets remember though that Bede only noted in his writings that the British referred to the same lunar month, which the Jews established for Passover, as Eostre-monath. He was equally clear that the former pagan religion was quite dead for some long time, and that the celebrations which occurred were quite

25

definitely Christian in origin.

The Date

Easter depends on Passover not only for much of its symbolic meaning but also for its position in the calendar; the Last Supper shared by Jesus and his disciples before his crucifixion was a Passover meal, based on the chronology in the Gospels. (See Appendix 2) As a result some of the early Christians always celebrated Easter on Nissan 14, the date of Passover each year. This is interesting because Jesus did not raise from the dead on Passover but rather two days later on the Feast of First Fruits on Nisan 16. Still, the early Bishops did choose to celebrate the resurrection on the day of Passover. However, the problem with Nisan 14 in the minds of some in the Western Church (who wished to further associate Sunday and Easter) is that it was calculated by the moon and could fall on any day of the week.

Every Sunday of the year is a commemoration of the Resurrection of Christ, which had occurred on a Sunday. Because the Sunday after 14 Nisan was the historical day of the Resurrection, at Rome this Sunday became the Christian feast of Easter. Easter was celebrated in Rome and Alexandria on the first Sunday after the first full moon after the spring equinox, and the Roman Church claimed for this observance the authority of Peter and Paul.

However, the Bishops of Asia Minor stood firm and a number of early bishops rejected the practice of celebrating Easter on the first Sunday after Nisan 14. They favored adhering to celebrating the festival on Nisan 14 in accord with the Biblical Passover and the tradition passed on to them by the Apostles. This conflict between Easter and Passover is often referred to as the "Paschal Controversy."

By the 3rd century the Church, which had become Gentile-dominated and wishing to further distinguish itself from Jewish practices, began a tone of rhetoric against Nisan 14 or Passover. The tradition that Easter was to be celebrated "not with the Jews" meant that Easter was not to be celebrated on Nisan 14.

A number of ecclesiastical historians, primarily Eusebius and Bishop Polycarp of Smyrna, by tradition a disciple of John the Evangelist, disputed the computation of the date with Bishop Anicetus of Rome in what is now known as the Quartodecimanism controversy. The term *Quartodeciman* is derived from Latin, meaning fourteen, and refers to this practice of fixing the celebration of Passover for Christians on the 14th day of Nisan.

Shortly after Anicetus became bishop of the church of Rome in the mid second century (ca. AD 155), Polycarp visited Rome and among the topics discussed was when the pre-Easter fast should end. Neither Polycarp nor Anicetus was able to convert the other to his position. Both could claim Apostolic authority for their traditions, but they did not consider the matter of sufficient importance to justify a schism, so they parted in peace leaving the question unsettled.

Irenaeus, who observed the "first Sunday" rule notes of Polycarp, "For Anicetus could not persuade Polycarp to forgo the observance [of his Nisan 14 practice] inasmuch as these things had been always observed by John the disciple of the Lord, and by other apostles with whom he had been conversant." Irenaeus notes that this was not only Polycarp's practice, but that this was the practice of John the disciple and the other apostles that Polycarp knew. Also based on the writings of Irenaeus, the Roman church had celebrated Passover on a Sunday at least since the time of Bishop Sixtus I, 115-125 A.D. (3).

In the end, a uniform method of computing the date of Easter was not formally settled until the First Council of Nicea in 325, although by that time the Roman timing for the observance had spread to most churches. The Council came to a decision that the Church as a whole should use a unified system, which was the Roman one. They decided in favor of celebrating the resurrection on the first Sunday after the first full moon following the vernal equinox, independently of the Bible's Hebrew Calendar, and authorized the Bishop of Alexandria to announce annually the exact date to his fellow bishops. This duty fell on this officiate because of the resources at Alexandria he could draw on. The precise rules to determine this are very involved, but the Resurrection is usually the first Sunday after a full moon occurring no sooner than March 21, which was the actual date of the vernal equinox at the time of the First Council of Nicaea.

Easter in the Early Church

The observance of any non-Jewish special holiday throughout the Christian year is believed by some to be an innovation postdating the Early Church. The ecclesiastical historian Socrates Scholasticus (b. 380) attributes the observance of Easter by the church to the perpetuation of local custom, "just as many other customs have been established," stating that neither Jesus nor his Apostles enjoined the keeping of this or any other festival (4). However, when read in context, this is not a rejection or denigration of the celebration—which, given its currency in Scholasticus' time would be surprising—but is merely part of a defense of the diverse methods for computing its date. Indeed, although he describes the details of the Easter celebration as deriving from local custom, he insists the feast itself is universally observed. Perhaps the earliest extant primary source referencing Easter is a 2nd century Paschal homily by Bishop Melito of Sardis, which characterizes the celebration as a well-established one (see Appendix #3). (5).

The Easter Season

The Customs of Easter were begun in the earliest days of church history. As time passed and the church grew ever larger. More and more Easter customs were added. After the Reformation and the beginning of the Protestant Churches most of the Easter customs were no longer celebrated. In today's churches the Protestant celebration is usually very brief while the Catholic, Orthodox and Episcopal Churches continue with extensive observations of the season. It is important for us to understand that, however we choose to celebrate the Season of the Resurrection of Christ most of these customs have been celebrated by the church for centuries and most have their roots deeply embedded in a desire to get closer to to the Lord and worship Him more fully.

In Western Christianity, Easter marks the end of the forty days of Lent, a period of fasting and penitence in preparation for Easter which begins on Ash Wednesday. Today most protestant denominations do not celebrate an Easter *Season*, however more and more churches are celebrating at least some part of the historical Eastertide. As we will see below, many of our spiritual and cultural customs come from these historical celebrations of Easter.

Historically and traditionally in Western Christianity, Lent is the forty-day period (or season) lasting from Ash Wednesday to Easter or Holy Saturday. Lent is also a time of preparation for Holy Week, which recalls the events linked to the Passion of Christ and culminates in the celebration of the Resurrection of Jesus Christ.

Holy Week begins with Palm Sunday and there are remembrances on Maundy Thursday, Good Friday, in many churches the Easter Vigil on the Saturday before Easter, and then of course, Easter Sunday. Many Protestant churches do not celebrate any of these days except Palm Sunday and Easter Sunday. Sometimes they include a sunrise service on Easter morning. To see the full Easter Season Schedule according to the plans of all the church combined (see Appendix #4).

Easter Today

Despite the religious preeminence of Easter, in many traditionally Christian countries Christmas is now a more prominent event in the calendar year, being unrivaled as a festive season, commercial opportunity, and time of family gathering — even for those of no or only nominal faith. Easter's relatively modest secular observances place it a distant second or third among the less religiously inclined where Christmas is so prominent.

Throughout North America and parts of the UK, the Easter holiday has been partially secularized, so that some families participate only in the attendant revelry, central to which is decorating Easter eggs on Saturday evening and hunting for them Sunday morning, by which time they have been mysteriously hidden all over the house and garden. According to the children's stories, the eggs were hidden overnight and other treats delivered by the Easter Bunny in an Easter basket which children find waiting for them when they wake up. The Easter Bunny's motives for doing this are seldom clarified. Many families in America will attend Sunday services in the morning and then participate in a feast or party in the afternoon. In the UK, the tradition has boiled down to simply exchanging chocolate eggs on the Sunday, and possibly having an Easter meal; it is also traditional to have hot cross buns.

Easter eggs are a popular sign of the holiday among its religious and secular observers alike. Although claims are often made that Easter Eggs were originally pagan symbols, there is no solid evidence for this; the one source for information on a possible pagan Goddess who may have given her name to the festival, Eostre, does not mention eggs at all, and as there is no other available information on Eostre, there is no apparent connection to eggs. It is not until the 18th Century that Jakob Grimm (German philologist, jurist and mythologist, best known as a recorder of fairy tales, one of the Brothers Grimm) theorized a pagan connection to Easter Eggs, this time with a goddess of his own making whom he named Ostara, a suggested German version of Eostre.

At the Passover Seder, a hard-boiled egg dipped in salt water symbolizes both new life and the Passover sacrifice offered at the Temple in Jerusalem. In Christian times, the egg had bestowed upon it a religious interpretation, becoming a symbol of the rock

28

tomb out of which Christ emerged to the new life of His resurrection. It can also represent the darkness inside the tomb inside a hollow egg. The egg is symbolic of the grave and life renewed by breaking out of it. The egg itself is a symbol of the Resurrection while being dormant it contains a new life sealed within it.

The Easter egg tradition may have also celebrated the end of the privations of Lent. In the West, eggs were forbidden during Lent as well as other traditional fast days. Likewise, in Eastern Christianity, both meat and dairy are prohibited during the fast, and eggs are seen as "dairy" (a foodstuff that could be taken from an animal without shedding its blood).

How Does the Resurrection Affect Us?

If we believe in the evidence of the resurrection of Jesus Christ as recorded in the New Testament, what significance does the resurrection have for us?

In the resurrection of Jesus Christ we see the clear demonstration of the power of the true God. Ephesians 1:19-21 tells us that it is the power of our heavenly Father that raised Jesus Christ from the dead.

The resurrection proves that Jesus Christ is God. That is exactly what God the Father wanted to communicate to us, as we read in Romans 1:4. The Jews crucified Jesus Christ because, to them, he was blaspheming when he said that he was the Son of God, equal to the Father. The resurrection of Jesus Christ demonstrates the truth that he is who he said he was.

Our salvation depends on our faith in the resurrection of Jesus Christ. In Romans 10:9, we are told how to be saved. It says that "if you confess with your mouth 'Jesus is Lord' and believe in your heart that God raised him from the dead, you will be saved." This means that you cannot be a Christian unless you believe in the resurrection of Jesus Christ. This should tell us that even if some people are in churches, if they reject the resurrection of Jesus Christ, they are not Christians.

The resurrection of Jesus Christ demonstrates to us that all the teachings of Jesus Christ are true. Everything Jesus taught was true, including his great promise in John 6:40, "Everyone who looks to the Son and believes in him shall have eternal life, and I will raise him up on the last day." Jesus' teachings concerning his person, his work, heaven, hell, and the future judgment are all true.

The resurrection of Jesus Christ secured our justification. "Christ died for our sins and he was raised for our justification," Paul says in Romans 4:25.

Our own resurrection depends completely on the resurrection of Jesus Christ. Read 1 Thessalonians 4:14: "We believe that Jesus died and rose again and so we believe that God will bring with Jesus those who have fallen asleep in him." There are a number of other verses concerning this, including 2 Corinthians 4:14, and others.

The power for our Christian life in the present is the power of his resurrection. We read about this in Ephesians 1:19-21, as well as in Romans 6:4: "We were therefore buried with him through baptism into death in order that, just as Christ was raised from the dead through the glory of the Father, we too may live a new life." People ask me, "How can we live this Christian life?" We can live it by the same power that raised Jesus Christ from the dead.

The resurrection of Jesus Christ demonstrates that this Jesus Christ is going to be the appointed judge of all the wicked people in the world. In Acts 17:31, Paul told the Athenians, "'For he [God] has set a day when he will judge the world with justice by the man he has appointed. He has given proof of this to all men by raising him from the dead.'" We see the same idea in John 5:22 where Jesus said, "Moreover, the Father judges no one, but has entrusted all judgment to the Son." In verses 27-29 he continued, "And he has given him authority to judge, because he is the Son of Man. Do not be amazed at this, for a time is coming when all who are in their graves will hear his voice and come out-- those who have done good will rise to live, and those who have done evil will rise to be condemned." The resurrection of Jesus Christ means that he will raise up everyone who ever lived--some to eternal life and some to eternal damnation--and Jesus Christ will be the judge of the wicked. All who have trusted in their fallen reason and rejected the claims of Jesus Christ will be raised up from the dead by Jesus Christ himself. He will judge and damn them.

Conclusion

Because of the miracle of Christ's resurrection, Jesus' depressed and disappointed disciples were instantly transformed. They began to preach the gospel with power, and the resurrection of Jesus was at the heart of their preaching. Why? Without the resurrection, there is no Christianity. These disciples of Jesus willingly suffered martyrdom for their faith and the enemies of the Gospel were totally unable to refute this central claim of the gospel. They could not produce the body of Jesus Christ and put a stop to Christianity. The Jewish believers, meanwhile, were so impressed by this miracle that they began to worship on the day of Christ's resurrection, Sunday, rather than on Saturday, as their custom and their culture had been.

Footnotes for Chapter Three

1- Robert Hamerton-Kelly. *Spring Time: Seasons of the Christian Year.* p. 113.

2- Larry Boemler. *Asherah and Easter*, Biblical Archaeology Review, Vol. 18, Number 3, 1992-May/June.

3- Eusebius. *Ecclesiastical History.* Chapters 23 to 25

4- Nicene/Post-Nicene, Series II, Volume 26 - Socrates Scholasticus

5-. Kerux: The Journal of Northwest Theological Seminary. *Homily on the Pascha.* Retrieved on 2007-03-28.

6- www.orthodox.net/greatlent/synaxarion-sunday-of-last-judgment-meatfare sunday

7- Dr. Peter Toon. *From Septuagesima to Quadragesima*. www.lent.classicalanglican

8- Marguerite Ickis. *The Book of Religious Holidays and Celebrations.* p. 110.

9- Schaff, Philip. *The Author's Views respecting the Celebration of Easter, Baptism, Fasting, Marriage, the Eucharist, and Other Ecclesiastical Rites. Socrates and Sozomenus Ecclesiastical Histories*. Retrieved on 2007-03-28.

Chapter Four – Tisha B'Av
The Fast of the Fifth Month
July (Av 9)

2 The people of Bethel had sent Sharezer and Regem-Melech, together with their men, to entreat the LORD 3 by asking the priests of the house of the LORD Almighty and the prophets, "Should I mourn and fast in the fifth month, as I have done for so many years?" 4 Then the word of the LORD Almighty came to me: 5 "Ask all the people of the land and the priests, 'When you fasted and mourned in the fifth and seventh months for the past seventy years, was it really for me that you fasted? (Zechariah 7:2-5)

Five misfortunes befell our fathers ... on the ninth of Av....On the ninth of Av it was decreed that our fathers should not enter the [Promised] Land, the Temple was destroyed the first and second time, Bethar was captured and the city [Jerusalem] was ploughed up. (Mishnah Ta'anit 4:6)

In the fifth month, on the seventh day of the month ...came Nebuzaradan ... and he burnt the house of the L-RD...(II Kings 25:8-9)

In the fifth month, on the tenth day of the month... came Nebuzaradan ... and he burnt the house of the L-RD... (Jeremiah 52:12-13)

How then are these dates to be reconciled? On the seventh the heathens entered the Temple and ate therein and desecrated it throughout the seventh and eighth and towards dusk of the ninth they set fire to it and it continued to burn the whole of that day. ... How will the Rabbis then [explain the choice of the 9th as the date]? The beginning of any misfortune [when the fire was set] is of greater moment. (Talmud Ta'anit 29a)

"Jesus answered, and said unto them, Destroy this temple, and in three days I will raise it up. Then said the Jews, Forty and six years was this temple in building, and wilt thou raise it up in three days? But he spoke of the temple of his body." (John 2:19-21)

"I am come that they might have life, and that they might have it more abundantly." (John 10:10b)

"Blessed is he whose transgression is forgiven, whose sin is covered." (Psalm 32:1)

Tisha B'Av and the Truth of Consequences
by Sara Yoheved Rigler

Joan, a once-beautiful, recovering alcoholic, stood up at an AA meeting and told her story:

I married Jeff, my high school sweetheart, and we had two kids. I started drinking when our kids were little, but Jeff had no idea. I used to hide the bottles in very clever hiding places, and I drank vodka, so he never smelled it on my breath.

But then my drinking got worse. Often I couldn't get up in the morning to get the kids off to school because of a hangover, so Jeff found out. He warned me that if I didn't stop, I'd destroy our family. I thought he was just threatening and I didn't listen to him. My drinking got worse. Jeff told me, over and over again, that he would divorce me if I didn't go on the wagon. But you have to understand that he was crazy about me and always had been, so I knew he'd never do it.

Then, in the middle of the night one night, I woke up from a drunken stupor. I must have been out for a long time, maybe the whole previous day. I looked around and discovered that Jeff and the kids were gone. I mean really gone. They had moved out and taken all their stuff with them. I couldn't believe it. Jeff was always crazy about me. I was sure he'd come back. I was sure until the day the divorce papers arrived by registered mail. Then I knew that I had ruined my life. That's when I started to come to AA.

Unheeded Warnings

Tisha B'Av marks the day when God walked out on the Jewish people, and took His house with Him. Like the husband in this true story, He had warned them over and over again. Like the wife in this story, they were convinced that His love for them would keep Him with them forever. But they continued to indulge in destructive actions, heedless of their effect on them and on their union with the Almighty.

Then one day -- the ninth day of the Hebrew month of Av -- God did exactly what He had said He would do. He permitted the Jew's enemies to destroy the Holy Temple, which had been the resting place for the Divine Presence in this physical world, and He removed Himself from their lives.

The Jews of ancient Judea had never known life without God in their midst. The Temple of Solomon had dominated their existence for almost 400 years. Daily life in Jerusalem revolved around the Temple service, and even those who resided far away were obligated to make the pilgrimage to the Temple three times a year. Life without the Temple and the Divine immanence it represented was completely inconceivable.

The terrible day the Temple went up in flames was a day of defeat and death, of calamity and consternation. Yet the prevailing emotion, more than horror or grief, was disbelief. Just as Joan could not believe that her husband had really left her, so too the Jewish people -- even after 150 years of Prophetic warnings -- could not believe that God had really left them.

~~~~~~

Tisha B'Av (lit. "Ninth of Av") is another rabbinically instituted holiday that God didn't mandate. However, it is an important fast day to the Jewish people. It is a day of national mourning. Tisha B'Av, the Fast of the Ninth of Av, is a day of mourning to commemorate the many tragedies that have befallen the Jewish people, many of which providentially have occurred on the ninth of Av. Av on the Jewish calendar occurs on our August/September (see Appendix #2).

Tisha B'Av primarily commemorates the destruction of the first and second Temples, both of which were destroyed on the ninth of Av about 656 years apart, but on the same date (the first by the Babylonians in 586 B.C.; the second by the Romans in 70 A.D.). Although this holiday is primarily meant to commemorate the destruction of the Temple, it is appropriate to consider on this day the many other tragedies of the Jewish people, which occurred on this day all through history. Most notably in the Middle Ages for example, the expulsion of the Jews from Spain in 1492. The Alhambra Decree, issued March 31, 1492, ordered all Jews to leave Spain by the end of July 1492. July 31, 1492 was Tisha B'Av.

Tisha B'Av is the culmination of a three week period of increasing mourning in connection with the fall of Jerusalem, beginning with the Tenth of Tevet, when the siege began; the Seventeenth of Tammuz, when the first breach was made in the wall; and the Third of Tishrei, known as the Fast of Gedaliah, the day when Gedaliah was assassinated (II Kings 25:25; Jeremiah 41:2). Gedaliah was the Governor of Israel during the days of Nebuchadnezzar King of Babylonia. As a result of Gedaliah's death the final vestiges of Judean autonomy after the Babylonian conquest were destroyed, many thousands of Jews were slain, and the remaining Jews were driven into final exile.

During this three week period, weddings and other parties are not permitted, and people refrain from cutting their hair. From the first to the ninth of Av, it is also customary to refrain from eating meat. The restrictions on Tisha B'Av are similar to those on Yom Kippur: to refrain from eating and drinking (even water); washing, bathing, shaving or wearing cosmetics; wearing leather shoes; engaging in sexual relations; and studying Torah (because this was viewed as a pleasurable activity). Work in the ordinary sense of the word (rather than the Sabbath sense) is also restricted. People who are ill need not fast on this day. Many of the traditional mourning practices are observed: people refrain from smiles, laughter and idle conversation, and sit on low stools. In synagogue, the book of Lamentations is read and mourning prayers are recited. The ark (cabinet where the Torah is kept) is draped in black.

After the Destruction of the Temple

The loss of the Temple had been a traumatic experience for the Jewish people, and insistent efforts were made to perpetuate its memory. Pilgrimages to Jerusalem were maintained long after the Temple's loss. These took place on Tisha B'Av and on the three pilgrim feasts. Prayer became a substitute for sacrifice, and rituals were adopted to reinforce the symbolic link between the Temple and the Synagogue. There was also a revision of the Haggadah to include reference to the Passover Sacrifice at the Temple and prayers for the restoration of Jerusalem (1).

When the Temple stood, Jerusalem was the bustling capital of Jewish activity and the focal point of all Jewish existence. At least 3 times a year, wherever they were, Jews would come to Jerusalem in honor of the pilgrim festivals. Jerusalem was also the seat of the Sanhedrin (the High Court) and the center of Jewish learning. The Holy City united the Jewish people and focused all their physical and spiritual endeavors towards God.

Today, although the Temple no longer stands, Jerusalem is still the focal point of

Jewish existence. Numerous customs reflect the significance of Jerusalem in our lives. At the festive occasion of a Jewish wedding, a glass is shattered in memory of Jerusalem, and it is customary to leave part of one's house unpainted in honor of the Temple. These customs and many more permeate our daily existence. During the 3 weeks, the customs of mourning intensify as we commemorate the period when Jerusalem was besieged and the Temple razed to the ground.

From Zechariah 7:5, 8:19 it appears that after the building of the Second Temple the custom of keeping these fast-days was temporarily discontinued. Since the destruction of Jerusalem and of the Second Temple by the Romans, the four fast-days have again been observed.

The Five Calamities

According to the Mishnah (Taanit 4:6), five specific events occurred on the ninth of Av that warrant fasting:

The twelve scouts sent by Moses to observe the land of Canaan returned from their mission. Two of the scouts, Joshua and Caleb, brought a positive report, but the others spoke disparagingly about the land which caused the Children of Israel to cry, panic and despair of ever entering the "Promised Land." For this, they were punished by God that their generation would not enter the land. Because of the Israelites' lack of faith, God decreed that for all generations this date would become one of crying and misfortune for their descendants, the Jewish people. (See Numbers Ch. 13–14)

The First Temple built by King Solomon and the Kingdom of Judah was destroyed by the Babylonians led by Nebuchadnezzar in 586 BC and the Judeans were sent into the Babylonian exile (Daniel 1:1).

The Second Temple was destroyed by the Romans in 70 AD, as Jesus predicted in Luke 19:43-44 scattering the people of Judea and commencing the Jewish exile from the Holy Land.

Following the Roman siege of Jerusalem, the razing of Jerusalem occurred the next year. According to the Talmud in tractate Taanit, the destruction of the Second Temple began on the ninth and was finally consumed by the flames the next day on the Tenth of Av.

Bar Kokhba's revolt against Rome failed in 135 CE. Simon bar Kokhba was killed, and the city of Betar was destroyed. As the prophet Jeremiah predicted, Jerusalem was ploughed over - on the ninth of Av.

Turnus Rufus   ploughs the site of Temple and the Romans build the pagan city of Aelia Capitolina on site of Jerusalem.

The Roman Emperor Hadrian established a heathen temple on the site of the Temple, one year later.

Calamities according to Tradition

According to the tradition, Aaron, the High Priest, died on this day. Aaron was known for his love of peace. It is thus paradoxical that in this month, a tragedy of overwhelming proportions befell the Jewish people, in part, the rabbis tell us, because of the inability of the Jewish community of Judea to maintain cordial relations with one another.

The people of Israel miscalculated the amount of time that Moses was meant to be on the mount, and on the 39th day of his absence (17th of Tammuz) fearing that he would not return, they built an idol - the golden calf. When Moses saw that the nation, who had just made a covenant with God, had built an idol, he was overcome by anger and he threw the 10 commandments to the floor, smashing them to pieces.

During the days of the destruction of the first Temple, the walls of the City of Jerusalem were breached on the 9th of Tammuz. Although the enemies entered the city and spread desolation, they were unable to enter the Sanctuary because the Priests had fortified themselves and continued to perform the daily offerings.

On the 13th of Tammuz, the Priests had no more sheep for the daily offering, so they bribed the besieging soldiers for gold and silver in return for sheep. On the 17th of Tammuz, the soldiers stopped sending up sheep and *for the first time, the daily offerings ceased.*

On the 17th of Tammuz, a number of years before the destruction of the Second Temple, during the time of the Roman Procurator Comenus, there was great tension between the Romans and the Jews. Josephus Flavious tells of the burning of the Torah Scroll by Comenus and his forces: "On the royal road, near Beit Horon, robbers befell the cortege of Stephanus, a royal official, and they thoroughly plundered it. Comenus sent an armed force to the nearby villages and ordered the arrest of their inhabitants, who were then to be brought before him. It was their sin that they failed to pursue and capture the robbers. One of the soldiers seized a scroll of the Holy Torah in one of the villages; he tore it and cast it into the fire... From all sides the Jews gathered in trembling, as if their entire land had been given to the flames..."

Some hold that Apustumus, a royal Roman official, placed an idol in the Second Temple on the 17th of Tammuz. (See Appendix 5 for the full account of the 17th of Tammuz.)

Later Calamities on the Ninth of Av

A large number of calamities also occurred on the ninth of Av:

In 1095 the First Crusade was declared by Pope Urban II. 10,000 Jews were killed in first month of Crusade. The Crusades brought death and destruction to thousands of Jews, totally obliterating many communities in Rhineland and France.

In 1190 there was the mass suicide of the Jews of York during the anti-Jewish riots of that year.

In 1290, King Edward I signed an edict to expel the Jews from England

On the 9th of Av 1492, the Jews were expelled from Spain.

Sabbatai Zevi, the false Jewish messiah, was born on Tisha B'av in 1626.

In the First World War, Germany declared war on Russia on August 1, 1914, Tisha B'av.

On July 31, 1941 coinciding with Tisha B'Av, under instructions from Adolf Hitler, Nazi official Hermann Göring ordered SS general Reinhard Heydrich to make all the necessary preparations for the Final Solution.

The 9th of Av 1942 - The first killings started at Treblinka: "The first transport of 'deportees' left Malkinia on July 23, 1942, in the morning hours. It was loaded with Jews from the Warsaw ghetto. The train was made up of sixty closed cars, crowded with people. The car doors were locked from the outside, and the air apertures barred with barbed wire."

Some calamities that occurred shortly before or after the ninth of Av:

In 1955, El Al Flight 402 was shot down over Bulgarian airspace on the 8th of Av.

The AMIA Bombing (Asociación Mutua Israelita Argentina) by terrorists in the city of Buenos Aires, which killed 85 and wounded more than 120, occurred on July 18, 1994, the 10th of Av.

The Gulf War began on August 2, 1990 - the 11th of Av - with the Invasion of Kuwait by Iraq. It ended on Purim.

The Second Lebanon War began on July 12, 2006, the 16th of Tammuz, and continued until 14 August 2006, the 20th of Av.

A Point of Interest

The destruction of the Temple, something that happened almost two thousand years, ago comes back to haunt the collective consciousness of the Jews as if it happened yesterday. This is what so impressed the French ruler Napoleon Bonaparte when he looked in on a synagogue in Paris on Tisha B'Av and saw Jews sitting on the floor chanting lamentations and shedding tears. After inquiring about the cause for their mourning and hearing that it was the destruction of their Holy Temple in Jerusalem he expressed astonishment that he had heard nothing about this tragedy from his reliable intelligence sources. When it was explained that this event took place close to 1800 years earlier he reportedly declared that a people who can still mourn for their Temple and their homeland after so many years have a real hope for regaining them (2).

The Future Tisha B'av

The name of the month of Av is of Babylonian origin. It is also called *Menachem*

Av ("The comforting of Av"), in anticipation of the consolation for which the Jew hopes, after all the misfortunes that happened. In the future, to that same degree that the ninth of Av has been a day of tragedy, it will be a day of great happiness. For, according to the Rabbis, on the 9th of Av, the Messiah will be born from the tribe of Judah. His coming will wipe the tear from every eye. If we do our part in committing ourselves to spiritual and moral change we can be sure that God will do His part and send the Messiah to return all of us to our land, rebuild the Temple and turn the sad day of Tisha B'Av into a day of celebration (3).

One of the Jewish commentaries ("Halakhot Gedolot") states, "Anyone who eats or drinks on Tisha B'Av will not see the (future) rejoicings of Jerusalem because it is written in Isaiah (66:10) 'Rejoice ye with Jerusalem … all ye that mourn for her.'"

Customs and Restrictions
Tisha B'Av is a fast day similar to Yom Kippur. While most other fasts on the Jewish calendar only last from dawn to nightfall, the Tisha B'Av fast lasts about 25 hours, beginning at sunset on the eve of Tisha B'Av and ending at nightfall the next day. Tisha B'Av also shares five additional prohibitions with Yom Kippur: no eating or drinking, washing or bathing, application of creams or oils, wearing of leather shoes or sexual relations or displays of physical affection

These restrictions are waived in the case of health issues. For example, those who are seriously ill may eat and drink, in contrast to Yom Kippur, when eating and drinking is allowed only in cases of life-threatening need. (On other fast days almost any medical condition may justify breaking the fast; in practice, since many cases differ, consultation with a rabbi is often necessary.) Ritual washing up to the knuckles is permitted. Washing to cleanse dirt or mud from one's body is also permitted.

Additional Customs Associated with Mourning
Torah study is forbidden on Tisha B'Av (as it is considered an enjoyable activity), except for sad texts such as the Book of Lamentations, the Book of Job, portions of Jeremiah and chapters of the Talmud that discuss the laws of mourning (4). From the meal immediately before the fast until noon the next day, it is customary to sit on low stools or on the floor, as is done during shiva (funeral mourning). If possible, work is avoided during this period. Electric lighting may be turned off or dimmed, and prayers recited by candlelight. Some sleep on the floor or modify their normal sleeping routine, by sleeping without a pillow, for instance. People refrain from greeting each other or sending gifts on this day. Old prayer books and Torahs are often buried on this day.

Customs During The Days Preceding And Following Tisha B'av
Three Weeks: During the Three Weeks from 17th Tammuz until the 9th of Av, the Jewish nation undergoes a collective period of mourning. Historically, the period between the 17th of Tammuz and the 9th of Av, has witnessed a series of calamities and disastrous events for world Jewry. During the mourning period, Jews focus on the destruction of the First and Second Temples, signifying the cessation of the national, social and political life of the Jewish state.

The prophets have promised that there will be a future time when Zion will be comforted from all the troubles that have befallen her since the destruction of the Second Temple. Until then, the Three Weeks is a period of mourning and reflection, which intensifies in the 9 days that count down to a dramatic close with the fast of Tisha B'Av. In the three weeks before Tisha B'Av, some Jews do not cut their hair or shave. Weddings are not held during this period.

The Nine Days: The days leading up to Tisha B'Av are known as The Nine Days. The Nine Days consists of those days leading up to the Fast of Ninth Av (Tisha B'Av). When the month of Av enters, the sages say, one should reduce one's level of happiness. Mourning customs are observed in deference to the memories of the two holy temples destroyed and the various other catastrophes that occurred on that day. Orthodox Jews refrain from eating meat during all or part of this period, and some refrain from pleasurable activities such as going to music concerts or swimming.

From the first of the month until the Fast of the Ninth of Av, it is customary to take on additional strictures regarding the mourning rites of the Three Weeks. These include the avoidance of music, merriment, and meat. It is also customary to refrain from drinking wine (5). A correspondence is thus drawn to the cessation of the Temple offerings and libations, as the destruction of the Sanctuary approached. Of course, overriding these restrictions are the special meals associated with a mitzvah, health problems or severe economic hardship.

Other restrictions for the Nine days are: Launder clothing (except for a baby's), wearing new or freshly laundered clothing. (Those who want to change their clothing daily should prepare a number of garments and wear each of them briefly before the onset of the Nine Days. Then it is permitted to wear them during the Nine Days), bathe for pleasure or swim, remodel or expand home, plant trees to be used for shade or fragrance (as opposed to fruit trees), buy, sew, weave, or knit new clothing, cut nails on the actual week of the fast of Tisha B'Av (starting from the Saturday night beforehand). The prayer "Levana" is recited after Tisha B'Av. There is no law forbidding traveling during the Nine Days; however it is customary to refrain from traveling (or engaging in any potentially perilous activity) during these days unless it is absolutely necessary.

Shabbat Chazon: The Sabbath before Tisha B'Av is called *Shabbat Chazon* (lit. "Shabbat of Vision"), alluding to the prophetic reading of the week, from the first chapter of the Book of Isaiah. In this prophecy, the Children of Israel are rebuked, but also comforted:

Zion will be redeemed with judgment
And those that return to her with righteousness.

Although the fast ends at nightfall, it is customary to refrain from eating meat and drinking wine until noon of the following day. According to tradition, the Temple burned all night and most of the day of the tenth of Av (6).

Services

The scroll of Lamentations is read in synagogue during the evening services. In addition, most of the morning is spent reading "dirges", most bewailing the loss of the Temples and the subsequent persecutions, but many others referring to post-exile disasters. These later dirges were composed by various poets (often prominent Rabbis) who had either suffered in the events mentioned or relate received reports. In many Sephardic congregations the Book of Job is read on the morning of Tisha B'Av.

History of the Observance

In the long period, which is reflected in Talmudic literature the observance of the Ninth Day of Av, assumed a character of constantly growing sadness and asceticism. By the end of the second century or at the beginning of the third, the celebration of the day had lost much of its gloom. Rabbi Judah ha-Nasi was in favor of abolishing it altogether or, according to another version, of lessening its severity when the fast has been postponed from Saturday to Sunday (7). The growing strictness in the observance of mourning customs in connection with the Ninth Day of Av became pronounced in post-Talmudic times, and particularly in the darkest period of Jewish history, from the fifteenth century to the eighteenth.

In Today's World

Rabbi Yirmiyahu Ullman says "we mustn't think that the absence of the Temple is a result of the shortcomings of prior generations, and no fault of our own. The Sages taught, "Any generation in which the Temple is not built, it is as if it had been destroyed in their times" (*Yerushalmi, Yoma 1a*). The same lack of merit resulting in its destruction has resulted in its not being rebuilt. In fact, the Midrash states a frightening outcome of not yearning for the rebuilding of the Temple, "All the communities that fell, it is only because they didn't inquire after and demand the *Beit HaMikdash*" (Temple) (*Midrash Socher Tov, Shmuel 31*). What can we do to demonstrate our interest in, and increase our merit that the Temple be rebuilt? The Rabbis taught, "Those who study about the Temple, it is as if the Temple was built in their days" (*Menachot 111a*). Accordingly, the main way to enhance our feeling of loss, and also to demonstrate our desire that the Temple be rebuilt, is through study (8).

Jesus in Tisha B'Av

Although Tisha B'Av has no prophetic or Messianic significance, the Bible does speak of all fast days being turned into days of joy, gladness, and cheer. Zechariah 8:19 says "This is what the LORD Almighty says: "The fasts of the fourth, fifth, seventh and tenth months will become joyful and glad occasions and happy festivals for Judah. Therefore love truth and peace." When Jesus the Messiah returns to establish His rule and reign on the Earth, the sadness of Israel will be turned to joy, and there will be no need for Tisha B'Av or any other fast days of mourning. Until that glorious day of Messiah's return, we, as believers in Him, while being mindful of the gravity of this day, must seek to bring the Gospel message to those who are fasting and mourning so their sadness may turn into gladness and joy!

In Luke 3:4-6 we hear John the Baptist preaching. He was probably preaching on the Sabbath after Tisha B'Av because he was preaching from Isaiah 40:3-5 which says: *As is written in the book of the words of Isaiah the prophet:" A voice of one calling* *in the desert, `Prepare the way for the Lord, make straight paths for him. Every valley shall be filled in, every mountain and hill made low. The crooked roads shall become straight, the rough ways smooth. And all mankind will see God's salvation.' "* Now Isaiah 40:1-26 is the passage of Scripture read from the scroll of the prophets on the first Sabbath after Tisha B'Av. There are seven readings from Isaiah between Tisha B'Av and Rosh Hashanah. These passages span from Isaiah 40 through Isaiah 63. After Jesus' baptism, His forty days of fasting in the desert, and time spent preaching in the synagogues in the Galilee, His return to His hometown synagogue in Nazareth would have marked the end of seven week period between Tisha B'Av and the Sabbath before Rosh Hashanah.

The destruction of Solomon's Temple by the Babylonians was a judgment of God due to the sin of the nation of Judah (9). More than a century earlier, the Northern Tribes were taken into captivity by Assyria for their idolatries. It is interesting to note that the second Temple (Herod's Temple) was destroyed on the first day of the week, the day of the week when Christ rose from the dead (10)! John's crying out in the wilderness was a call to repentance and spiritual preparation for the coming Messiah Jesus. It was initiated on a day of great mourning and fasting.

Seven weeks later, Jesus, whose name means salvation, read from Isaiah the Prophet, whose name means God is Salvation. Jesus read from Isaiah 61 verse one and the first half of verse two which says: *"The Spirit of the Sovereign LORD is on me, because the LORD has anointed me to preach good news to the poor. He has sent me to bind up the brokenhearted, to proclaim freedom for the captives and release from darkness for the prisoners. to proclaim the year of the LORD's favor."* He proclaimed the year of the LORD's favor, but did not go on to pronounce the "day of God's vengeance."

Rosh Hashanah commences the Ten Days of Awe. These ten days are the most solemn and introspective on the Hebrew Calendar. They mark the days between the New Year and the Day of Atonement. Yom Kippur is the most holy, most solemn day for the Jewish people. It is the last day of the High Holy Days, which began on Rosh Hashanah. Many Jewish people spend the entire day in the synagogue, praying and fasting in the hope that their sins will be forgiven and that they will be written in the Lamb's Book of Life for the coming year.

Tisha B'Av was the day that John the Baptist proclaimed that he was a voice crying out in the wilderness. It was a day of mourning and fasting. It was a call to turn from sin. Jesus proclaimed that He was the Messiah on the Sabbath before the Ten Days of Awe. These days of repentance culminated on Yom Kippur. Yom Kippur is a day set aside to "afflict the soul," to fast and pray.

Jesus is the Anointed On. He is the Messiah. He was anointed to preach the good news, the gospel. He was sent to set the captives free. He is the one who transformed Tisha B'Av from a day of mourning to a day of joyous salvation!

Footnotes for Chapter Four
1- Abba Eben. *The Story of the Jews.* p. 113.

2- www.ohr.edu/yhiy/article.php/1130

3- Ibid.

4- Hayim Halevy Donin. *To Be a Jew*. p. 264.

5- Alfred J. Kolatch. *The Jewish Book of Why*. p. 287.

6- Ibid. p. 265.

   (The laws of Tisha B'Av are recorded in the Shulkhan Arukh (the "Code of Jewish Law") *Orach Chayim* 552-557.)

7- (Talmud, Tractate Megillah 5b).

8- www.ohr.edu/yhiy/article.php/2296

9- Kevin Howard and Marvin Rosenthal. *The Feasts of the Lord*. p. 153.

10- Alfred Edershiem. *The Temple*. p. 218.

Chapter Five – The Sabbatical Year (Including the Jubilee Year)

The year following the destruction of the second Holy Temple (3829 from creation, equivalent to 68-69 AD) was the first year of the seven-year Sabbatical cycle. We continue counting seven from then. This is also Rosh Hashanah.

1 The LORD said to Moses on Mount Sinai, 2 "Speak to the Israelites and say to them: 'When you enter the land I am going to give you, the land itself must observe a sabbath to the LORD. 3 For six years sow your fields, and for six years prune your vineyards and gather their crops. 4 But in the seventh year the land is to have a sabbath of rest, a sabbath to the LORD. Do not sow your fields or prune your vineyards. 5 Do not reap what grows of itself or harvest the grapes of your untended vines. The land is to have a year of rest. 6 Whatever the land yields during the sabbath year will be food for you—for yourself, your manservant and maidservant, and the hired worker and temporary resident who live among you, 7 as well as for your livestock and the wild animals in your land. Whatever the land produces may be eaten. (Lev. 25:1-7 – see Appendix #6)

1 At the end of every seven years you must cancel debts. 2 This is how it is to be done: Every creditor shall cancel the loan he has made to his fellow Israelite. He shall not require payment from his fellow Israelite or brother, because the LORD's time for canceling debts has been proclaimed. 3 You may require payment from a foreigner, but you must cancel any debt your brother owes you. 4 However, there should be no poor among you, for in the land the LORD your God is giving you to possess as your inheritance, he will richly bless you, 5 if only you fully obey the LORD your God and are careful to follow all these commands I am giving you today. 6 For the LORD your God will bless you as he has promised, and you will lend to many nations but will borrow from none. You will rule over many nations but none will rule over you.

7 If there is a poor man among your brothers in any of the towns of the land that the LORD your God is giving you, do not be hardhearted or tightfisted toward your poor brother. 8 Rather be openhanded and freely lend him whatever he needs. 9 Be careful not to harbor this wicked thought: "The seventh year, the year for canceling debts, is near," so that you do not show ill will toward your needy brother and give him nothing. He may then appeal to the LORD against you, and you will be found guilty of sin. 10 Give generously to him and do so without a grudging heart; then because of this the LORD your God will bless you in all your work and in everything you put your hand to. 11 There will always be poor people in the land. Therefore I command you to be openhanded toward your brothers and toward the poor and needy in your land. (Deut. 15:1-11)

What Is The Sabbatical Year?

The seventh year, during which the fields were to be left fallow (Leviticus 25:1-7) and debts released (Deuteronomy 15:1-11) is called in Hebrew *Shemitah* ("Release"). The seven years are counted in the cycle of fifty culminating in the Jubilee and are known by tradition. The year 2000/2001, for instance, was a Sabbatical year. In order to avoid the cancellation of all debts, a serious hardship in our commercial society today, a device called the Prosbul was introduced even in Talmudic times of handing the debts over before the end of the Sabbatical year, to a temporary court consisting of three persons, the debts then being considered to have been paid to the court beforehand. The Sabbatical Year and Jubilee Year provided for a period of both social equality and ecological recovery.

Most of the Sabbatical year's observances are agricultural in nature, and are only relevant in Israel. For those in the Diaspora, the Sabbatical year has two practical ramifications: a) Produce which is imported from Israel must have Rabbinical Certification and is also subject to certain laws and restrictions due to their sanctity. b) The laws of debt absolution are in effect in all locations. Needless to say, the spiritual and hallowed nature of this special year is applicable and pertinent worldwide.

The problem of agricultural work in the Sabbatical year did not arise in modern times until, under the impact of Zionism, colonies were established in Palestine; it is a severe difficulty now that the State of Israel has been established. The more Orthodox do observe the laws of the Sabbatical year, using only agricultural products bought from Arabs, or imported.

What Is The Jubilee Year?

Jubilee is the institution described in the book of Leviticus (25:8-24) where it is stated that a series of forty-nine years was to be counted (there is considerable uncertainty as to the date from when the counting is to begin, but traditionally it is from the creation of the world) and every fiftieth year declared a special year during which there was to be no agricultural work; all landed property was to revert to its original owner; and slaves were to be set free. The name Jubilee is from the Hebrew word *yovel*, ("ram's horn"), the year being so called because a ram's horn was sounded when it was proclaimed (Leviticus 25:9). Since this verse says: *"Proclaim liberty throughout the land for all its inhabitants,"* the Talmudic view is that the Jubilee was not observed during the Second Temple period because the majority of Jews no longer lived in the land of Israel (1).

What Are The Biblical Commands For These days?

The people were to observe the seventh year, during which the land is to lie fallow, and also the celebration of the fiftieth year after seven Sabbatical cycles. So important was the law regarding the Jubilee that, like the Decalogue, it was ascribed to the legislation on Mount Sinai (Lev. 25:1). It was to come into force after the Israelites should be in possession of Palestine: *"When ye come into the land which I give you"*. The law provides that one may cultivate his field and vineyard six years, but *"in the seventh year shall be ... a Sabbath for the Lord,"* during which one shall neither sow nor reap as hitherto for his private gain, but all members of the community—the owner, his servants, and strangers—as well as domestic and wild animals, shall share in consuming the natural or spontaneous yield of the soil (2).

The fiftieth year after that following the last year of seven Sabbatical cycles, is the Jubilee; during it the land regulations of the Sabbatical year are to be observed, as is also the commandment *"ye shall return every man unto his possession"* (*Lev. 25:*10), indicating the compulsory restoration of hereditary properties (except houses of laymen located in walled cities) to the original owners or their legal heirs, and the emancipation of all Hebrew servants whose term of six years is unexpired or who refuse to leave their masters when such term of service has expired (3). The regulations of the Sabbatical year include also the annulment of all monetary obligations between Israelites, the creditor being legally barred from making any attempt to collect his debt (Deut. 25:1). The law for the Jubilee year does not have this provision.

Technically the Talmud distinguishes the Sabbatical year for the release or quitclaim of loans - money-release, in distinction to the land-release. There is also a difference in that money loans are not annulled until the end of every seven years, as the Mosaic Law permits, but the land-release begins with the seventh year (4).

What Were The Reasons for Observing Sabbatical Year and Jubilee Year Laws?

1- Rest from labor is an absolute necessity both for animal and for vegetable life because continuous cultivation will eventually ruin the land. The law of the Sabbatical year also acts also as a statute of limitation for a bankruptcy law for the poor debtor, in discharging his liability for debts contracted, and in enabling him to start life anew on an equal footing with his neighbor, without the fear that his former creditors will seize his future earnings.

The Jubilee year was also the year of liberation of servants whose poverty had forced them into employment by others. Similarly all property that had been sold or leased for a money consideration in order to relieve poverty, was to be returned to the original owners without restoration of the lease or sale amount, which had been advanced.

2- The Rabbinical view stated that these laws were made to promote the idea of theocracy: that one year in seven might be devoted "to the Lord," as the weekly Sabbath is devoted to rest from manual labor and to the study of the Law.

3- This year is also for making up for six years of Sabbaths. Some Rabbis taught that the Sabbatical Year enabled the *field* to rest. It is true that we rest on the Sabbath, but even as we rest, our fields continue to work. We plant on Friday and the seeds continue to germinate on the Sabbath. During the Sabbatical Year our fields make up for the lost Sabbaths and festivals of the previous six years.

4- The Sabbatical Year is a lesson in faith and humility. The laws of the Sabbatical Year were only binding upon our ancestors after they settled in Israel. When we toil and labor over crops that we grow, or other forms of income that we generate, we can grow proud of our achievements and take personal credit for them. We are liable to forget that God's blessing is the sole reason for our success. We are liable to forget that God gave us our land and our seed, that He made the rain fall, the sun shine and the crops grow. The Sabbatical Year reinforces our faith in God's providence over our affairs.

5 - The Sabbatical Year demonstrates unity. It is easy to share with others when we can afford to share, when we have a steady income and when we know how we will pay for tomorrow's expenses. It is much more difficult to be charitable when we are unsure of what tomorrow holds. Landowners had no income during the Sabbatical Year, yet they would routinely abandon to the public all crops that grew spontaneously during this year. In this way the Sabbatical Year enhanced Jewish unity.

6- The Sabbatical Year reveals our liberation. The belief that the world belongs to God and that our success depends on him is a liberating notion. It enables us to release the burdens that we carry. We still toil, but we breathe easier. We still labor, but we sleep easier. We know that God guides our footsteps and that everything happens for a good reason. We learn to see God's hand in everything we do and His presence in everything we see.

7- The Talmud informs us that in the Holy Temple the Levites sang God's praises every day. On the Sabbath, the seventh day, they sang about the day of eternal rest, the messianic age. The Talmud teaches that our world will last for six millennia. The first two were devoted to creation. The second two were devoted to Torah. The last two are devoted to the Messiah. Indeed, the Talmud tells us that in the seventh millennium, the world, as we know it will cease to exist. It will become a world of freedom and of Godliness. The Sabbatical Year - the seventh year, like the Sabbath - the seventh day, represents the messianic age. Our faith in God is strengthened during the Sabbatical Year, just as it will be in the messianic age. Our unity is strengthened during the Sabbatical Year, just as the messiah will usher in an age of peace. The sixth year is a year of plenty just as the messiah will usher in an age of prosperity. The messianic age is most notably known for freedom. Indeed, the Sabbatical Year is a year of emancipation. Slaves are liberated and all debts are cleared (5). (See Appendix #7.)

8- The Jubilee was instituted primarily to keep intact the original allotment of the Holy Land among the tribes, and to relieve the idea of servitude to men. *"For unto me the children of Israel are servants; they are my servants"* (Lev. 25:55); and they shall not be servants to servants, as God's bond has the priority (6). That the main object was to keep intact each tribe's inheritance is evident from the fact that the Sabbatical and Jubilee years were not inaugurated before the Holy Land had been conquered and apportioned among the tribes and their families. The first Sabbatical year is said to have occurred twenty-one years after the arrival of the Hebrews in Palestine, and the first Jubilee year thirty-three years later (7).

The Jubilee was proclaimed "throughout all the land unto all the inhabitants thereof," however, only when all the tribes were in possession of Palestine was the Jubilee observed. It was not observed after the tribes of Reuben and Gad and the half-tribe of Manasseh had been exiled; nor was it observed during the existence of the Second Temple, when the tribes of Judah and Benjamin had been assimilated. After the conquest of Samaria by Shalmaneser the Jubilee was observed nominally in the expectation of the return of the tribes until the final exile by Nebuchadnezzar (8).

Where are the Sabbatical Year and Jubilee Year Observed?

The area of the Holy Land over which the Sabbatical Year was in force included at the time of the First Temple all the possessions of the Egyptian emigrants, which territory extended south to Gaza, east to the Euphrates, and north to the Lebanon Mountains. Ammon and Moab in the southeast were excluded. In the period of the Second Temple the area of the Babylon emigrants, headed by Ezra, was restricted to the territory west of the Jordan and northward as far as Acre. The Rabbis extended the Sabbatical year to Syria, in order not to tempt settlers of the Holy Land to emigrate there.

46

The area of Palestine was divided into three parts, Judea, Galilee, and the Transjordan districts, where the Sabbatical year existed in more or less rigorous observance.

What was the Duration of the Sabbatical Year and Jubilee Year?

The duration of the Sabbatical year was from autumn to autumn, beginning with New-Year's Day (Rosh Hashanah); but as a precaution against any infringement of the Law, the Rabbis extended the time and prohibited sowing and planting thirty days before Rosh Hashanah. Still later they prohibited the sowing of grain from Passover, and the planting of trees from Pentecost preceding the Sabbatical year, in order not to derive any benefit from the fruits bearing in that year. The extension of the time is known as "preceding the seventh". The penalty for non-observance of the Sabbatical year is exile; for eating the fruits of the seventh year (*i.e.*, of the sixth year's growth), pestilence. The duration of the Jubilee year was from autumn to autumn, beginning with New Year's Day (Rosh Hashanah).

Rabbinical Extensions Concerning Finances

The Rabbinical enactment extended the money-release aspect of the Sabbatical year to countries other than the Holy Land, but confined the land-release aspect to Palestine within Ezra's boundary lines of occupation during the period of the Second Temple. The money-release was obviously independent of the Holy Land and was intended to free from his debts the poor in every land, and at a certain period of time. On the other hand, this bankruptcy law checked all business enterprises, which the Jews were engaged in, after they had largely abandoned agricultural pursuits. Hillel the Elder then amended the law by his institution of the *Prosbul.* In addition to this subterfuge, there are various exceptions which exclude the following debts: wages, merchandise on credit, loans on pledges, a note guaranteed by mortgage, one turned over for collection and one which stipulates that the debtor waives the Sabbatical Year defense as regards this particular note (even though he can not waive the law in general).

The money-release aspect of the Sabbatical year was undoubtedly intended for the poor debtor, though the rich man also might take advantage of the general law. The Mishnah, however, plainly expresses the Rabbis' satisfaction with the debtor who does not make use of the Sabbatical year in order to be relieved of his obligations. Maimonides, in his *Responsa*, rules that the Sabbatical Year is not operative against orphans, but that all other debts are wiped out. The Rabbis nevertheless desired that the law of the Sabbatical year should not be forgotten (9).

The money-release aspect of the Sabbatical year is relaxed in Palestine today. The principal reasons seem to have been that the fixed date of payment, the guaranty attached, and the terminology of the present-day notes abrogate the law of the Sabbatical year. The Sabbatical year land-release, however, has been generally observed in Palestine; and during the Sabbatical year the Jews of the Holy Land eat only of the products grown in the Transjordanic districts (10) (See Appendix 8).

Talmudic and Samaritan Calculation of Jubilees

The exact year of the Sabbatical year is in dispute, and different dates are given. According to Talmudic calculations the entrance of the Israelites into Palestine occurred in the year of Creation 2489, and 850 years, or seventeen Jubilees, passed between that date and the destruction of the First Temple. The first cycle commenced after the conquest of the land and its distribution among the tribes, which, occupied fourteen years, and the last Jubilee occurred on the "tenth day of the month Tishri, in the fourteenth year after that the city was smitten" (Ezek. 40:1), which was the New-Year's Day of the Jubilee. Joshua celebrated the first Jubilee, and died just before the second.

The Samaritans in their "Book of Joshua" date the first month of the first Sabbatical cycle and of the first Jubilee cycle as beginning with the crossing of the Jordan and the entrance of the Israelites into their possession; and they insist that the date was 2794 of Creation, according to the chronology of the Torah "and the true reckoning known to the sages since the Flood" (11).

The First and the Second Temple, the Talmud says, were destroyed on the closing of the Sabbatical year. The sixteenth Jubilee occurred in the eighteenth year of Josiah, who reigned thirty-one years; the remaining thirteen years of his reign, together with the eleven years of those of Jehoiakim and Jehoiachin and the eleven years of that of Zedekiah (II Kings 25), fix the first exilic year as the thirty-sixth year of the Jubilee cycle, or the twenty-fifth year of the captivity of Jehoiachin, or fourteen years from the destruction of the Holy City.

The Babylonian captivity lasted seventy years. Ezra sanctified Palestine in the seventh year of the second entrance, after the sixth year of Darius, when the Temple was dedicated (Ezra 6:15, 16, 7:7). The first cycle of Sabbatical year began with the sanctification of Ezra. The Second Temple stood 420 years, and was destroyed, like the First, in the 421st year, on the closing of the Sabbatical year.

Various Dates

The Talmud gives as a rule for finding the Sabbatical year to add one year and divide by seven the number of years since the destruction of the Second Temple, or to add 2 for every 100 years and divide the sum by seven. The difference among the Jewish authorities as to the correct Sabbatical year is due to the varied interpretation of the words "closing of Shabbat," as meaning either the last year of the cycle or the year after the cycle; also as to the beginning of the exilic Sabbatical year from the year when the destruction of the Temple occurred, or from the year after.

Maimonides gives the date of a Sabbatical year occurring in his time as the year 1107 from the destruction of the Temple, 1487 of the Seleucidan era, 4936 of Creation (= 1175 AD); *i.e.*, he begins the cycle with the year following that of the destruction. The Sabbatical year was finally settled according to the view of Maimonides, which agreed with the most plausible interpretation of the correct Talmudic text and also with the practice of the oldest members of the Jewish communities in the Orient by whom the Sabbatical years were observed. Evidence to this effect was given at a conference of Rabbis called in Jerusalem, who concurred in the opinion expressed by the Rabbis from Safed, Damascus, Salonica, and Constantinople fixing the Sabbatical year of their time as 5313 = 1552 AD (12).

The Sabbatical Year in Historical Evidence

Herod Captures Jerusalem: Josephus describes the capture of Jerusalem by Herod the great. The repeated mention of a Sabbatical year at this time has been problematic for chronologists. Josephus describes the siege and capture of Jerusalem by Herod during the latter half of the first century B.C. First he describes the siege, during the summer before Jerusalem fell. He plainly states that the Jews at that time "were distressed by famine and the want of necessaries, for this happened to be a Sabbatic Year." (Ant. 14.475) Then he describes the capture of Jerusalem on the Day of Atonement, Tishri 10 which would have been in the autumn of the year.

Famines: Famines caused by the Sabbatical year were fairly common after the capture of Jerusalem by Herod. On the other hand, there seems to be no mention in the historical record of a famine caused by the Sabbatical year prior to the capture of Jerusalem.

Deacons: The first Deacons of the Church were appointed during a time when food was scarce. A dispute about unequal distribution of necessities (specifically food) caused the Apostles to appoint seven Deacons to be in charge of distribution to Greek Christians specifically their widows and poor. (Acts 6:1ff). The most likely time for such a dispute would be during a Jewish Sabbatical year, when the Jews would neither sow nor harvest their crops (Lev 25:1-7). Looking at the times of the Sabbatical years it is most likely that the date for the appointment of the first Deacons was in A.D. 21.

Missions: In Acts 11:27-30; 2:25, Saul and Barnabas are sent to Judea during a famine (Acts 11:28), during the reign of Claudius (Acts 11:28), and about the time of the death of Herod Agrippa I (Acts 12:1-23). Their purpose is to bring relief to the brethren of Judea. This famine was also mentioned by Josephus (Ant. 20.51), not long after he mentions the death of Herod Agrippa I (Ant. 20.1). Herod Agrippa I died in the third year of the reign of Claudius, after his own reign of seven years. In historical chronology, the third year of Claudius' reign was A.D. 28, which was also a Sabbatical year.

When is the next Jubilee year?

In short, the answer to your question is that the Jubilee year is currently not observed or commemorated (13). According to Biblical law, the Jubilee is only observed when all Twelve Tribes of the Jewish nation are living in Israel, as is learned from the verse (Leviticus 25:10). *"And you shall sanctify the fiftieth year, and proclaim freedom throughout the land for all who live on it,"* which implies that the Jubilee is only sanctified when "all who live on it" -- meaning all who are meant to be living there -- are in the Land of Israel. Furthermore, the Jubilee is only observed when every tribe is living in the specific part of the land which was it was allotted when the Land of Israel was divided.

In approximately 720 BC, the Assyrians conquered the Northern Kingdom of Israel and sent the majority of its population into exile. Before that point in time the Jubilee was regularly observed. We also know that with the destruction of the Second Temple and the disbandment of the *Sanhedrin* (Supreme Rabbinical Court) we ceased to mark the Jubilee year in any form. With the exile of the Northern Kingdom the required condition for the Jubilee to be sanctified was lost. Thus, the last time there was a Biblical requirement to observe the Jubilee was about 150 years before the destruction of the First Temple.

"When is the next Jubilee year?" We eagerly await the day when God will bring our entire nation back to our homeland -- including the ten "lost" tribes -- and we will again resume observing the Jubilee year (14).

Christianity and the Sabbatical Year

There is evidence that the concept and practice of the Sabbatical year had an influence upon the origins of early Christianity. Based upon calculations of the known Roman period Sabbatical cycles, it is hypothesized that the origins of the ministries of Jesus and John the Baptist may have dovetailed with a Sabbatical year and created the types of hardships for the poor that had earlier forced Hillel to reconstitute the meaning of remission of loans and created the legal fiction of the "prosbul."

In addition, Jewish tradition tied the observance of the Sabbatical year to the coming of the messiah and so the emphasis upon the poor and the meaning attached to the sermons of Jesus may have had even greater significance in the Sabbatical year cycles. This originally suggested a ministry of only one year, but later was interpreted as the announcement of a Jubilee year. Jesus read from Isaiah, *"The Spirit of the Lord is upon Me, Because He anointed Me to preach the gospel to the poor. He has sent Me to proclaim release to the captives, and recovery of sight to the blind, to set free those who are downtrodden, to proclaim the favorable year of the Lord." (Luke 4:18-19)* The words of Isaiah continue, "and the day of vengeance of our God." (Isa. 61:2) Was Jesus proclaiming a one-year ministry and/or a Jubilee year? What is the connection of Isaiah's words proclaiming the "day of vengeance?"

What the evangelist is telling us is that the long-awaited Jubilee Year is here with Jesus now. This is the year of God's favor, the moment that inaugurates an overturning of structures that keep people bound, replacing it with a sense of solidarity among all. Jesus stepped directly into the captivity of the human experience. He accepted the constrictions of our broken humanity. But he transformed the scourges of our human condition with love. Those who had been held captive by prejudice were liberated by his acceptance. Those who were blind because of sin came to a new sense of vision with the forgiveness they had received from him.

Conclusion

The ultimate object of these times of rest and refreshing and restoration was so that man could receive a foretaste of the time of refreshing and rest, which will occur when the Messiah comes. Jesus declared that He was the one who fulfilled messianic prophecy (Luke 4:17-21) which many believe is a direct proclamation that Jesus ushered in the coming of the Kingdom of Heaven and the true year of Jubilee. He is coming to restore everything that has been destroyed by sin since the beginning of the world, to abolish all slavery and to establish true liberty for the children of God (Acts 3:19-21, Romans 8:19-23 and Matthew 25:31-34 (15).

Footnotes for Chapter Five

1- Rabbi Louis Jacobs. *The Jewish Religion: A Companion.* Excerpts.

2- Isidor Grunfeld. *Shemittah and Yobel: Laws referring to the Sabbatical Year in Israel and Its Produce.* p. 2.

3- (Gen. 18: 6; 'Ar. 33b; see Josephus, "Ant." vi. 8, & 28).

4- (Sanh. v. 1).

5- Talmud. *Rosh Hashanah.* 31a.

6- Sifra, Behar Sinai, 7. 1. {The Sifra is a Jewish Commentary on Leviticus that is connected to the Midrash which is a Jewish Commentary on the traditions of the Rabbis}

7- Ibid. 1. 3.

8- Ibid. 33a

9- Maimonides. *Responsa - Pe'er ha-Dor.* No. 127.

10- Schwartz. *Tebu'at ha-Are.* p. 20.

11- Raphael Kirchheim. *Karme Shomeron.* p. 63.

12- R. Eleazar Azkari, "Sefer Hasidim," ed. Warsaw, 1879, p. 83.

13- Rabbi Baruch S. Davidson. *Encyclopedia Talmudit vol. XXII.* "Yovel" entry. (Although the laws of the Sabbatical Year are observed in Israel to this very day, the Jubilee year is not designated or observed. There are many reasons for this. Some of them: a) The Jubilee only affected the Sabbatical Year cycle when the Sabbatical Year was established and declared by the *Sanhedrin*, as opposed to today when it is automatically programmed into the perpetual Jewish calendar. b) The observance of the Sabbatical Year today is only a rabbinic decree, and therefore the Jubilee year does not affect its cycle. c) No commemoration is in order when there is no *Sanhedrin*, whose participation in the declaration of the Jubilee year was integral. In fact, it was the *Sanhedrin's* blast of the *shofar* (ram's horn) on Yom Kippur, which signaled the entry of the Jubilee year.)

14- Ibid.

15- William Curtis. *The Forgotten Feast.* p. 55.

Chapter Six – Advent
Four Sundays Before Christmas Day

O come, O come, Emmanuel, And ransom captive Israel,
That mourns in lonely exile here until the Son of God appear.
Rejoice! Rejoice! Emmanuel shall come to thee, O Israel.

O come, Thou Wisdom from on high, who orderest all things mightily;
To us the path of knowledge show, And teach us in her ways to go.
Rejoice! Rejoice! Emmanuel shall come to thee, O Israel.

O come, Thou Day-spring, come and cheer our spirits by Thine advent here;
Disperse the gloomy clouds of night, and death's dark shadows put to flight.
Rejoice! Rejoice! Emmanuel shall come to thee, O Israel.

O come, Desire of nations, bind, in one the hearts of all mankind;
Bid Thou our sad divisions cease, and be Thyself our King of Peace.
Rejoice! Rejoice! Emmanuel shall come to thee, O Israel.

First Sunday of Advent Scripture: *"In the beginning was the Word and the Word was with God and the Word was God. He was in the beginning with God. All things were made through Him and without Him nothing was made that was made. In Him was life, and the life was the light of men. And the light shines in the darkness, and the darkness did not comprehend it." (John 1:1-5)*

Second Sunday of Advent Scripture: *"The voice of one crying in the wilderness "Prepare the way of the Lord; Make straight in the desert a highway for our God. Every valley shall be exalted, and every mountain and hill brought low. The crooked places shall be made straight and the rough places smooth. The glory of the Lord shall be revealed, and all flesh shall see it together; for the mouth of the Lord has spoken." (Isaiah 40:3-5)*

Third Sunday of Advent Scripture: *Even Elizabeth your relative is going to have a child in her old age, and she who was said to be barren is in her sixth month. For nothing is impossible with God." "I am the Lord's servant," Mary answered. "May it be to me as you have said." Then the angel left her. (Luke 1:36-3)*

Fourth Sunday of Advent Scripture: *"So it was that while they were there, the days were completed for her to be delivered. And she brought forth her first born Son, and wrapped Him in swaddling cloths, and laid Him in a manger because there was no room for them in the inn." (Luke 2:7)*

The Four Sundays of Advent
The First Sunday: The first Sunday of Advent has the theme of *"Waiting"*. The Scriptures say that *"in the fullness of time"* the Messiah came to earth. So also, in the fullness of time will the Messiah come to earth the second time. In both times, all God's creation and all God's people were and are waiting for the salvation, redemption and eternal life promised by the Father.

This is also the Sunday of the *"Pre-existence of Christ."* When we celebrate the birth of Jesus we are not celebrating the beginning of His existence. Rather we are celebrating His first coming to earth as the Messiah. He has always existed. As one early church father put it, "There never was a time when the Son was not!"

The Second Sunday: The second Sunday of Advent has the theme of "Repentance and Preparation". As John the Baptist came before Jesus to call people to repentance, so we are called to turn back to God and make room in our hearts for Jesus. So let us during this week, return to the Lord, asking for His help, and asking for forgiveness. Jesus came so that we might be brought back to the Father.

The Third Sunday: The theme of the third Sunday of Advent Season is "Rejoicing". We are reminded that all those who are looking to Christ for salvation should give thanks and praise and rejoice - for our salvation has come! And we are reminded that when we come into the presence of Christ to live with Him for all eternity we will rejoice and sing "Alleluias" to Him as He sits on His throne in all His glory!

The Fourth Sunday: The theme of the fourth Sunday of Advent is "Salvation". The story of the Bible from Genesis to Revelation is how the Father provided salvation for His people through His Son, Jesus Christ. Advent reminds us of the time when the Lord Jesus came to earth to do the work of salvation. But it also reminds us that He is coming back again for all those who have received His salvation.

What is Advent About?

The word 'advent' is Latin for 'a coming or arrival'. The idea behind it is that God came to earthly life and lived among us, which is something to celebrate, because just by being in it, God was giving the supreme blessing to the created world. The focus of the entire season is the celebration of the birth of Jesus the Christ in his First Advent, and the anticipation of the return of Christ the King in his Second Advent. The general topic of Advent is the coming of Jesus Christ, both in the manger in Bethlehem and in the clouds of glory.

It is also a very important part of Advent to remember that this birth led to an execution of this same God on behalf of us, and then the greatest news - that death will not end it all! So it's not something you just go rushing into. We need to take stock of what that baby Jesus was here for. When we see the baby and the birth, the adult Jesus and His execution and resurrection are also in sight.

Advent, therefore, is a time of waiting, conversion and of hope. It is a time of waiting because it is the remembering of the first, humble coming of the Lord in as a human being. It is a time of waiting for His final, glorious coming as Lord of All and the Universal Judge. It is a time of conversion because the birth of Jesus leads to the cross through the message of John the Baptist, *"Repent for the kingdom of heaven is at hand"* (Mt 3:2). And it is the joyful hope that the salvation already accomplished by Christ (Rom. 8:24-25) and the reality of grace in the world, will mature and reach their fullness, thereby granting us what is promised by faith, and *"we shall become like Him for we shall see Him as He really is"* (John 3:2).

So, Advent is far more than simply marking a 2,000 year old event in history. It is celebrating a truth about God, the revelation of God in Christ whereby all of creation might be reconciled to God. That is a process in which we presently participate, and the consummation of which we anticipate. Scripture reading for Advent will reflect this emphasis on the Second Advent, including themes of accountability for faithfulness at His coming, judgment on sin, and the hope of eternal life. In the west, during the Middle Ages, Advent became a time to prepare for the Second Coming, because in those days, many people were convinced that all the signs pointed to the imminent return of Christ

In this double focus on past and future, Advent also symbolizes the spiritual journey of individuals and a congregation, as they affirm that Christ has come, that He is present in the world today, and that He will come again in power. That acknowledgment provides a basis for Kingdom ethics, for holy living arising from a profound sense that we live "between the times" and are called to be faithful stewards of what is entrusted to us as God's people. So, as the church celebrates God's "in breaking" into history in the Incarnation, and anticipates a future consummation to that history for which *"all creation is groaning awaiting its redemption,"* it also confesses its own responsibility as a people commissioned to *"love the Lord your God with all your heart"* and to *"love your neighbor as yourself."*

In Advent, Christians relive a dual impulse of the spirit: on the one hand, they raise their eyes towards the final destination of their pilgrimage through history, which is the glorious return of the Lord Jesus; on the other, remembering with emotion his birth in Bethlehem, they kneel before His manger.

Christians are very sensitive to this season of the year, especially when seen as the memory of the preparation for the coming of the Messiah. We are deeply conscious of the long period of expectation that preceded the birth of our Savior. The faithful know that God sustained Israel's hope in the coming of the Messiah by the prophets. Indeed, we are awestruck at the prospect of the God of glory taking flesh in the womb of the humble and lowly Virgin Mary. The faithful are particularly sensitive to the difficulties faced by the Mary during her pregnancy, and are deeply moved by the fact that there was no room at the inn for Joseph and Mary, just as she was about to give birth to the Christ child.

The hope of Christians is turned to the future but remains firmly rooted in an event of the past. In the fullness of time, the Son of God was born of the Virgin Mary: *"Born of a woman, born under the law",* as the Apostle Paul writes (Gal 4: 4).

Protestants and Advent

Many Protestant Churches and Christians see the Advent Season as a device of the Catholic Church and of course the Catholic Church established it when there was only one church. During the Reformation and in many churches after that all things Christmas were banned as being pagan or "popish". In today's church world, though, many churches are discovering that it is possible to have fuller seasons of the church year and to celebrate the great events in the life of our Savior and still be true to their own theological distinctive.

In fact, the Advent season presents a unique opportunity to many Protestants. It's like the once-a-year conjunction of two planets: It brings a great mass of Bible-loving, praise-and-worshipping, extemporaneously praying born-again Protestant Christians into close contact with a big chunk of the historic church's worship. Even many non-liturgical Protestants don't think twice about joining in the season's rituals, old as well as new. They pull out and count off advent calendars, listen to lectionary sermon themes and Bible readings, and recite set prayers at the dinner table around candles in meaningful hues of purple and rose. Advent's four bright Sundays offer us ways to meditate on Christ's coming, which is not limited to any one church, for joyous worship. Advent is a time of year that can "tie our lives to Christians throughout history." In a time of year filled with indulgence, the observance of centuries-old Christian practices can feed us in a deeper and better way.

What better source of encouragement for celebrating Advent as Protestants than Martin Luther the father of the Protestant Reformation. John Pless tells us a little about Luther and Advent. "For whatever reason, in the ineffable wisdom of God, the speech of Martin Luther rang clear where others merely mumbled.'" The clarity of Luther's voice is surely apparent in his Advent and Christmas preaching - the Lord's Palm Sunday entry into Jerusalem, the preaching of John the Baptist, the annunciation, and the nativity. Showing remarkable theological insight and pastoral warmth, Luther crafts vivid and graphic pictures of the meanness and misery of the biblical stories of the Lord's birth. *All* the great themes of Luther's theology - incarnation, justification, the "happy exchange," sacraments, the theology of the cross - are present in these sermons. Advent and Christmas evoke the best in Luther's preaching as he proclaims Bethlehem's crib in light of the cross. Ulrich Asendorf rightly notes "Luther's Advent sermons are a microcosm of his spiritual world" ('Ulrich Asendorf, "Luther's Sermons on Advent as a Summary of His Theology,"). Luther's preaching in Advent and Christmas is extensive. No less than 110 of Luther's Advent and Christmas sermons have been preserved. Roughly half of these sermons are based on Luke 2:1-20, although he clearly delighted in preaching the prologue of the Fourth Gospel as well" (1).

What is Advent?

Advent is a season of preparation. So's Lent, but it is a different kind of preparation. In Lent, each of us prepares for what happened on Good Friday (execution) and Easter (resurrection). Lent is very adult and serious, because it leads to a death. In fact, originally, Lent readied new Christian adults for baptism.

In Advent, we thank God for Christ's first coming, prepare for his final coming at the end of time, and celebrate Christ's presence among us today through His Spirit. God loved and wanted to share that love. But this existence isn't fit for God; it's too broken, evil, painful, and unjust. So, to rescue the created world from this evil, God chose to come here and walk the earth, to grow up, to live the truth, and to die. The only way to start such a thing is as a baby, and the only way to be a baby is to be born; hence Christmas. Because Christmas is centered in the new hope brought by a baby, it's a very child-oriented holiday. Because Advent leads us up to that baby, so also Advent is very child-oriented.

There's a time to get ready by focusing on your own sinfulness and evil, a time for personal transformation and following Christ to the cross; that's Lent. There's a time to get ready by rejoicing that our God is not far away and unfamiliar with the struggles of human life, that Christ is here right now among His followers, that God has already begun to bring in the Kingdom, and that Christ will come again to make it clear who really "reigns and rules" over the universe. That's Advent. "Lo, I am with you, even unto the end of the age", says Jesus. Christians intuitively understand that it is not possible to celebrate the birth of Him "who saves His people from their sins" without some effort to overcome sin in one's own life, while waiting faithfully for Him to return at the end of time.

So Advent originally was a time of fasting and self-reflection (instead of today's Christmas parties) and thinking about other people for a change. In the mid-300s, two events changed that thinking: Constantine the Great built the Church of the Nativity in Bethlehem, declaring Jesus' birthday a national holiday; and Julius, Bishop of Rome, set the date as December 25. Christmas took on a happier, more celebratory feel and became a time of joyous anticipation. By the mid-400s, even the Eastern Church—with a few exceptions—recognized December 25 as Christmas. However, Advent is still a much more solemn occasion among Orthodox Christians, and the season begins much earlier— November 15 instead of the Sunday nearest November 30. Still, it was not long after this that Christmas had greatly overshadowed Advent.

When is Advent?

Advent is the beginning of the Church Year for most churches in the Western tradition. It begins on the fourth Sunday before Christmas Day, which is the Sunday nearest November 30, and ends on Christmas Eve (Dec 24). If Christmas Eve is a Sunday, it is counted as the fourth Sunday of Advent, with Christmas Eve proper beginning at sundown. The liturgical season of Advent marks the time of spiritual preparation by the faithful before Christmas. While no special feast is prescribed, prayers and liturgical services stress preparation for the Lord's nativity (2).

In the U.S., most people start their Christmas after Thanksgiving Day (the fourth Thursday of November), though catalog firms and retailers try to move it up to the start of November for profit's sake. Thanksgiving day is actually quite appropriate for Advent, even if it is a few days before the season starts. Advent is a preparation, and the best way to start preparing is with a thankful heart.

History

The celebration of Advent has evolved in the spiritual life of the Church. In its earliest form, beginning in France (as we find from Venerable Bede's history), Advent was a period of preparation for the feast of the Epiphany, a day when converts were baptized; so the Advent preparation was very similar to Lent with an emphasis on prayer and fasting which lasted three weeks and later was expanded to 40 days.

In 380, the local Council of Saragossa, Spain, established a three-week fast before Epiphany. Inspired by the Lenten regulations, the local Council of Macon, France, in 581 designated that from Nov. 11 (the feast of St. Martin of Tours) until Christmas, fasting would be required on Monday, Wednesday and Friday. Eventually, similar practices spread to England. In Rome, the Advent preparation did not appear until the sixth century, and was viewed as a preparation for Christmas with less of a penitential bent (3).

The oldest document in which we find the length and exercises of Advent mentioned with anything like clearness, is a passage in the second book of the *History of the Franks* by St. Gregory of Tours, where he says that St. Perpetuus, one of his predecessors, who held that see about the year 480, had decreed a fast three times a week, from the feast of St. Martin until Christmas. It would be impossible to decide whether St. Perpetuus, by his regulations, established a new custom, or merely enforced an already existing law. We find, as far back as the fifth century, the custom of giving exhortations to the people in order to prepare them for the feast of Christmas.

Not many years after that, in 567, the second Council of Tours had enjoined the monks to fast from the beginning of December till Christmas. This practice of penance soon extended to the whole forty days, even for the laity: and it was commonly called St. Martin's Lent (this same council also proclaimed the twelve days from Christmas to Epiphany a sacred, festive season). Later on, in 582, the church ordained that during the same interval between St. Martin's day and Christmas, the Mondays, Wednesdays, and Fridays, should be fasting days, and that the Sacrifice should be celebrated according to the Lenten rite.

In 753 we see that Advent Fasts had spread into England, Italy, Germany and Spain. In the *capitularia* of Charles the Bald, in 846, the bishops admonish that prince not to call them away from their Churches during Lent or Advent, under pretext of affairs of the State or the necessities of war, seeing that they have special duties to fulfill, and particularly that of preaching during those sacred times. After this Advent was celebrated in all the Church in Western Christendom.

Since the 900s Advent has been considered the beginning of the Church year. This still does not mean that Advent is the most important time of the year, however. Easter has always had this honor.

How is Advent to be Observed?

The debate through out the church became when and how should Advent be celebrated. We have seen that it was started as a three week time of prayer and fasting that was later changed to 40 days. Soon this became the practice for the clergy and the laity. The discipline of the Churches of the west reduced the time of the Advent fast, and in a few years, changed the fast into a simple abstinence; and we even find the Councils of the twelfth century requiring only the clergy to observe this abstinence. The Council of Salisbury, held in 1281, would seem to expect none but monks to keep it. By degrees, the custom of fasting so far fell into disuse, that when, in 1362, Pope Urban V endeavored to prevent the total decay of the Advent penance, all he insisted upon was that all the clerics of his court should keep abstinence during Advent, without in any way including others, either clergy or laity, in this law.

In terms of worship, the Church gradually more and more formalized the celebration of Advent. Pope St. Gelasius I (d. 496) was the first to provide Advent liturgies for five Sundays. Later, Pope St. Gregory I (d. 604) enhanced these liturgies and Pope St. Gregory VII (d. 1095) later reduced the number of Sundays in Advent to four. Finally, about the ninth century, the Church designated the first Sunday of Advent as the beginning of the Church year (4).

The current form of Advent crystallized under Pope Gregory I, who set the current four-week length, and wrote liturgical materials for use in Advent. Later on, the church adopted a system of liturgical colors, and Advent received a purple color not unlike Lent's. The 20th century brought a rediscovery of joy in Advent preparations; this was signaled among Protestants who choose to celebrate this season of preparation by using the color blue (with or without a touch of red in it).

But Advent has fallen on hard times. For most people, it's become a time to get ready for whatever you're doing with family and friends on Christmas, and not a time to get ready for the Christ child. The bigger Christmas became, the more it swallowed up Advent. In fact, whatever Christmas-y thing we think of as being done before Christmas Day is actually done in Advent. In the US, everything after Thanksgiving is now seen as a part of Christmas. The main problem is not that Christmas intrudes on Advent. The real problem is that people no longer keep their *Christmas* focus on Christ, and then that Christless Christmas saps Christ from Advent. Practicing Advent as a religious season may help us recover Christmas, but it can't do it by itself. If you don't look to Jesus every day in every season, you'll lose Advent, Christmas, Lent, and even Easter. It'll be a tiring rush, not a loving celebration, and it'll be about family or money or image and not our loving Maker.   For the celebration of advent to be meaningful it must be focused on Christ alone.   Worship is the missing element in the monstrosity that the (Advent) Christmas Season has become.   We should worship as the Shepherds did – drop everything we are doing (today: we should participate in Advent prayer and fasting) and rush to the manger to attend His birth (Christmas)(5).

Commemorative Days in Advent

The primary *human* of the Advent Season according to the Western Church is Nicholas of Myra (modern Demre, Turkey) and his special day is on December 6. It was the celebration of his day and his reputation for giving gifts to children, which bred the name and task of Santa Claus. He apparently had very wealthy parents who died in one of the epidemics that were common back then. He got the inheritance, but started giving it away to the poor, the sick, children, and sailors. He was jailed for several years under the Emperor (as were most Christian leaders - if they weren't killed). When he was released, he was quite thin, but went right back to his giving ways. He was one of the bishops at the Council of Nicea in 325 and he died in 343 AD.

I mention him because of several interesting facts. First, while he was alive he was never associated with Advent or Christmas and all down through history, while he was associated with Advent and giving as Jesus gave, he was never associated with Christmas until the 19th Century. Secondly, Bishop Nicholas was a committed believer in Jesus Christ as his Savior and as the second person of the trinity, the very Son of God. He was at the council of Nicea to fight this very point and his side of the controversy won the day. Thirdly, Bishop Nicolas, at the council of Nicea helped to pick the date for the celebration of Easter, the celebration of the resurrection of the Lord. In his lifetime he never had anything to do with Advent or Christmas formally – such as setting dates, etc. So it is interesting that he is such a prominent part of the celebration of Christmas.

What started off as a tribute to Jesus through the dedicated life of one of His followers turned into a mythical, secular creature. We *must* keep our celebrations of Christ life, Christ centered or we too will turn them into the very opposite of what is intended – a time to reflect on the love and sacrifice of our Savior for us and on our eternal relationship with Him!

The Western Church has picked several other special people to remember during the Advent/Christmas season. The life of the disciple Thomas is remembered on December 21; it's a good day to think and pray about discerning, testing, and asking questions about what is happening around us, especially what's being taught about God. The day after Christmas (12/26) is the day to celebrate the life of the first Christian martyr, Stephen. This day was placed right after Christmas to remind us amidst our joy, of those who died to bring it to us. The beginning of the spread of the Gospel cost God's people their very lives. We never what to forget that – as the expression goes – "while salvation is free – it is not cheap"!

Conclusion

The Bible measures time by its content; the year when Isaiah had his great vision in the temple is not 746 BC, but it is the "Year in which King Uzziah died". And the time we enter upon now is not the current year, it is the time of God drawing near to His people, the time when the exile is ending and David's greater son the King/Messiah is drawing near. Therefore, get ready! Prepare in your hearts the way of the Lord, for this is the time of His coming (6)!

Footnotes for Chapter Six

1- John T. Pless. *Concordia Theological Quarterly: Learning to Preach from Luther in Advent and Christmas*. Volume 62: Number 4 October 1998.

2- Marguerite Ickis. *The Book of Religious Holidays and Celebrations*. p. 40.

3- Fr. William P. Saunders. *Catholic Herald*. 12/01/05 Issue

4- Ibid.

5- John MacArthur, Jr. *God With Us: The Miracle of Christmas*. p. 132.

6- Robert Hamerton-Kelly. *Spring Time: Seasons of the Christian Year*. p. 15.

Chapter Seven – Chanukah
December (Kislev 25)

Then came the Feast of Dedication at Jerusalem. It was winter, and Jesus was in the temple area walking in Solomon's Colonnade. The Jews gathered around him, saying, "How long will you keep us in suspense? If you are the Christ, tell us plainly."(John 10:22-24)

On the 25th of Kislev are the days of Chanukah, which are eight... these were appointed a Festival with Hallel [prayers of praise] and thanksgiving. (Shabbat 21b, Babylonian Talmud)

Our rabbis taught the rule of Chanukah: ... on the first day one [candle] is lit and thereafter they are progressively increased ... [because] we increase in sanctity but do not reduce. (Shabbat 21b, Babylonian Talmud)

"For eight days they celebrated the rededication of the altar. Then Judah and his brothers and the entire congregation of Israel decreed that the days of the rededication...should be observed...every year...for eight days. (1 Mac.4:56-59)" "the Jews celebrated joyfully for eight days as on the feast of Booths." (2 Mac.)
{Neither Jews or Protestants recognize the Book of Maccabees as part of the Bible.}

What is Chanukah?

The Feast of the Dedication of the Temple, Chanukah ('the dedication'), called in 1 Maccabees iv. 52-59 'the dedication of the altar,' and by Josephus (*Antiq.* xii. 7, 7) 'the Feast of Lights,' was another popular and joyous festival of the Jewish people that is still celebrated by them today. Chanukah, also known as the Festival of Lights, is an eight day festival beginning on the 25th day of the Jewish month of Kislev. It is an annual festival to honor the restoration of divine worship in the Temple after heathens had defiled it. The return of their religious liberty was to the Jews as life from the dead. So in remembrance of this new life, they kept an annual holiday on the twenty-fifth day of Kislev. Kislev is the third month of the Jewish calendar corresponding, approximately, to early December in the Gregorian calendar (See Appendix 2). The Bible tells us that Jesus kept this festival (John 10), however, the principal source for the story of Chanukah is found in the Talmud.

Interestingly, even though Chanukah is the most historically documented of the Jewish holidays, it is the only major Jewish holiday that has no basis in the Bible. Even though the Books of 1 & 2 Maccabees record the history of the Maccabees and the story of Chanukah for us, the Jews never considered these books as part of the Holy Scriptures. Rather, the Church preserved them along with other apocryphal books (1).

However, Chanukah is still, probably one of the best known Jewish holidays, and not because of any great religious significance, but because of its proximity to Christmas. Many non-Jews (and even many assimilated Jews!) think of this holiday as the Jewish Christmas, adopting many of the Christmas customs, such as elaborate gift giving and decoration. It is ironic that this holiday, which has its roots in a revolution against assimilation and the suppression of Jewish religion, has become the most assimilated, secular holiday on the Jewish calendar.

How did Chanukah come about?

Between the Old and New Testaments there are 400 years of which we know very little from the Bible. During the time of the Second Temple in Jerusalem, events took place that shook the world of God's people and the Jews today memorialize these events each year at Chanukah time. The Jewish people had returned to the Land of Israel from the Babylonian Exile, and had rebuilt the Holy Temple, but they remained subject to the reigning powers: first, the Persian Empire, then later, the conquering armies of Alexander the Great.

The story of Chanukah begins in the reign of Alexander the Great and ends by celebrating the cleansing of the Temple. Alexander conquered the world - and specifically for our story - Syria, Egypt and Palestine in 331 BC. However, he allowed the lands under his control to continue observing their own religions and to retain a certain degree of autonomy. Alexander was a kind and generous ruler to the Jews. He canceled the Jewish taxes during Sabbatical years, and even offered animals to be sacrificed on his behalf in the Temple. During the relatively benevolent years of Greek power, many Jews started to embrace the Greek Hellenistic culture adopting its language, customs and the dress as well as it's Hellenistic, pagan way of life. Later these same Jewish Hellenists helped with Antiochus Epiphanes' goal to abolish every trace of the Jewish religion.

After the death of Alexander, his kingdom was divided among his generals. One of these Generals was Ptolemy I who ruled Egypt and another was Seleucus who ruled North Syria and as far west as India. Down through the years, after these original generals had passed away, their descendants spent years fighting each other to gain more territories and power. Judea was caught in the middle and ended up under the system of the Seleucid Dynasty, Greek kings who reigned from Syria. Later, in 168 BC, while Antiochus Epiphanes of Syria was fighting with Egypt, Rome attacked Syria in the north. In order to defend himself from Rome, Antiochus had to withdraw from his war with Egypt.

Antiochus was so angry at having to withdraw from certain victory in Egypt, that while moving his army north he vented his fury against Israel, destroying much of the city of Jerusalem and slaughtering thousands of men, women and children. He began to oppress the Jews severely, placing a Hellenistic priest in the Temple, prohibiting the practice of the Jewish religion, and desecrating the Temple by requiring the sacrifice of pigs on the altar. He took all the treasures in the temple and forbid the Jews from keeping their holy traditions, such as the Sabbath, kosher laws, studying their holy books, and the practice of circumcision.

Many Jews changed their names from their Hebrew names, and followed the Greek "modern" practices, giving up the "old" ways of their ancestors. One Hellenized Jew's Hebrew name was Joshua, but he changed it to the Greek name Jason. He offered King Antiochus a bribe so he could take over the position of the High Priest. The "High Priest" Jason constructed a gymnasium near the Temple, and demoralized his fellow Jews with pagan customs and licentious behavior. Another Hellenized Jew came along and offered a bigger bribe and Jason was replaced.

Antiochus desecrated the Holy Altar by sacrificing a forbidden, unclean pig on it. The Temple was dedicated to the worship of Zeus Olympus and an altar to Zeus was set up on the high altar. The Jews were forced to bow before it under penalty of death. The Holy Temple was invaded, desecrated, and continually pillaged of all its treasures. Many innocent people continued to be massacred, and the survivors were heavily taxed. Antiochus went so far as to proclaim himself a god, taking the name Epiphanes - god manifest. The desecration of the Temple took place on Kislev 25.

In addition the Seleucids banned all temple practices, did away with the priests and sacrifices, outlawed all the festivals, and stopped all Jewish religious practices. Not only was circumcision banned but also circumcised babies were killed, and all the torahs they could find were burned. Then they went to every village and forced the people to sacrifice pigs on the village altars. With his residual army remaining in Israel Antiochus attempted to force the Jews to abandon Jerusalem and adopt the worship of the Greek gods. Many fled into the mountains; others cravenly complied.

"When the king had built an idol altar upon God's Altar, he slew swine upon it, and so offered a sacrifice neither according to the law, nor the Jewish religious worship in that country. He also compelled them to forsake the worship which they paid their own God, and to adore those whom he took to be gods; and made them build temples, and raise idol altars, in every city and village, and offer swine upon them every day (254). He also commanded them not to circumcise their sons, and threatened to punish any that should be found to have transgressed his injunction. He also appointed overseers, who should compel them to do what he commanded (255). And indeed many Jews there were who complied with the king's commands either voluntarily, or out of fear of the penalty that was denounced; but the best men, and those of the noblest souls, did not regard him, but did pay a greater respect to the customs of their country than concern as to the punishment which he threatened to the disobedient; on which account they every day underwent great miseries and bitter torments (256). For they were whipped with rods and their bodies were torn to pieces, and were crucified while they were still alive and breathed: they also strangled those women and their sons whom they had circumcised, as the king had appointed, hanging their sons about their necks as they were upon the crosses. And if there were any sacred book of the law found, it was destroyed; and those with whom they were found miserably perished also (2)."

There were two groups that opposed Antiochus: a basically nationalistic group led by Mattathias the Hasmonean and his son Judah Maccabee, and a religious traditionalist group known as the Chasidim, the forerunners of the Pharisees (no direct connection to the modern movement known as Chasidism). They joined forces in a revolt against both the assimilation of the Hellenistic Jews and oppression by the Seleucid Greek government. The revolution succeeded and the Temple was rededicated. (See Appendix #9.)

Mattathias, the Hasmonean, head of a priestly family, faithful to the Lord, and his five children, killed a group of Syrian soldiers who were in their village of Modine attempting to enforce the decree. The soldiers ordered him to sacrifice the pig or be killed. He refused to sacrifice the pig but before he could be killed another priest stepped forward and offered to kill the pig in order to save the village. Mattathias killed that priest and then he and his five sons killed all the soldiers. Knowing the Syrian army would come after them, they fled to the hills. Many people ran away from their villages all over Israel to escape from and fight against the Syrians. Many of those who had fled to the mountains joined with this godly family and began a campaign of gorilla warfare against the Syrian Army. During this time the Hasmoneans changed their name to "Maccabees" which means "the Hammer".

Three years to the day of its' desecration, on Kislev 25, 165 BC, the Maccabees and their followers had driven the Syrians from the Temple (later they drove them from Israel altogether). They regained control of the Holy Temple, and began the task of purifying it. The old polluted altar, which had been defiled by the sacrifice of a pig upon it, was torn down. They did not know what to do with the stones which were still precious to them, but now so polluted they could not be used. So the decided to stack them in a corner of the Temple complex to wait for Elijah or the Messiah to come and tell them what to do with them (3). Then taking unhewn stones, as the law commands, they built and consecrated a new altar on the model of the previous one.

They removed the Statue of Zeus, and the sacrifices and Priests were restored. All new holy vessels were crafted renewed and the lamp stand (the Menorah), and brought the Altar of Incense and the table of Shew bread into the Temple. They burnt incense on the Altar of Incense again and lit the lamps on the Menorah to shine within the Temple. They decorated the front of the Temple with golden wreaths and ornamental shields. They renewed the gates and the priest's rooms, and fitted them with doors. They consecrated the Temple courts and when they had put the Bread of the Presence on the table and hung the curtains, all their work was completed. Then the worship of the Lord was restored and a date for the rededication of the Temple was set – the twenty-fifth day of the Hebrew month of Kislev. The Temple was then rededicated to God with festivities that lasted eight days. The Maccabees ruled Judea until Herod took power in 37 BC. (See Appendix #10.)

What does Chanukah celebrate?

Chanukah is the celebration of that victory over Syria and the rededication of the Temple. It is an interesting celebration though because even though it is not commanded in Scripture it is a deeply spiritual celebration. It is apparent from history up to this point, that the triumph celebrated by Chanukah was a partial one at best. Although the Temple area had been liberated and the services re-instituted, parts of Jerusalem and nearly all the countryside were still under Syrian-Greek and Hellenistic control. Even the High Priest was a renegade Jew. Total independence only came many years later – but for that no festival was proclaimed.

That a festival was proclaimed in the absence of a military or diplomatic victory in any conventional sense of the word gives us an important insight into the nature of the celebration. Mattathias and Judah and his brothers risked their lives for spiritual freedom, the purity of the Temple and the integrity of its service, not for freedom from foreign bondage. They had been a vassal state ever since the Babylonian captivity, but when religious freedom was wrested from them they rebelled. When it was regained they celebrated (4).

Now this story does not include anything to do with oil or candles or lights. But because Judaism as a religion shies away from glorifying military victories, because the Hasmoneans later became corrupt, and because civil war between Jews (which occurred under later generations of Hasmoneans) is viewed as deplorable, Chanukah does not formally commemorate these historical events. Instead, Chanukah becomes a holiday focused on the Miracle of the Oil and the positive spiritual aspects of the Temple's rededication. The oil becomes a metaphor for the miraculous survival of the Jewish people through millennia of trials and tribulations. Chanukah was celebrated on Kislev 25 by the time of Jesus and interestingly, Kislev 25 on the Jewish Lunar calendar corresponds closely with our Solar calendar's December 25th.

The story of Chanukah is alluded to in the books of 1 and 2 Maccabees. But Chanukah is not actually mentioned, rather, a story similar in character, and obviously older in date, is the one alluded to in 2 Maccabees 1:18. This story is about the relighting of the altar-fire by Nehemiah due to a miracle which occurred on the twenty-fifth of Kislev, and which appears to be given as the reason for the selection of the same date for the rededication of the Temple altar by Judah Maccabeus.

The last day of Chanukah is known as *Zot Hanukkah*, from the verse in the Book of Numbers 7:84 "*Zot Chanukat Hamizbe'ach*" - "This was the dedication of the altar", which is read on this day in the synagogue. According to the teachings of Kabballah and Hasidism, this day is the final "seal" of the High Holiday season of *Yom Kippur*, and is considered a time to repent out of love for God.

The Eight Days

The version of the story in 1 Maccabees, states that an eight day celebration of songs and sacrifices was proclaimed upon rededication of the altar and the Temple, and makes no mention of the "Miracle of the Oil." The historian Josephus mentions the eight-day festival and its customs, but does not tell us the origin of the eight day lighting custom. Given that his audience was Hellenized Romans, perhaps his silence on the origin of the eight-day custom is due to its miraculous nature. In any event, he does report that lights were kindled in the household and the popular name of the festival was, therefore the "Festival of Lights" and it is called by this name to this day.

It has been noted that Jewish festivals are connected to the harvesting of the Biblical seven fruits which Israel was famed for. First Fruits is a celebration of the barley harvest, Pentecost of the wheat, Tabernacles of the figs, dates, pomegranates and grapes, and Chanukah of the olives. The olive harvest is in November and olive oil would be ready in time for Chanukah in December.

It has also been noted that the number eight has special significance in Jewish theology, as representing transcendence and the Jewish People's special role in human history. Seven is the number of days of creation, that is, of completion of the material cosmos, and also of the classical planets. Eight, being one step beyond seven, represents the Infinite. Hence, the Eighth Day of the Assembly festival, mentioned above, is according to Jewish Law a festival for Jews only (unlike Sukkoth, when all peoples were

64

welcome in Jerusalem). Similarly, the rite of circumcision, which brings a Jewish male into God's Covenant, is performed on the eighth day. Hence, Chanukah's eight days (in celebration of monotheistic morality's victory over Hellenistic humanism) have great symbolic importance for practicing Jews.

On each of the eight days the 'Hallel' was sung, the people appeared carrying palm and other branches, and there was a grand illumination of the Temple and of all private houses. These three observances bear so striking a resemblance to what we know about the Feast of Tabernacles, that it is difficult to resist the impression of some intended connection between the two, in consequence of which the daily singing of the 'Hallel,' and the carrying of palm branches was adopted during the Feast of the Dedication, while the practice of Temple-illumination was similarly introduced into the Feast of Tabernacles (In point of fact, the three are so compared in 2 Maccabees x. 6, and even the same name applied to them, i. 9, 18.)

All this becomes the more interesting, when we remember, that the date of the Feast of the Dedication - 25th of Kislev – was adopted by the ancient Church as that of the birth of our Lord, which would be the Dedication of the true Temple, the body of Jesus (John 2:19).

What is the Miracle of the Oil?

After 70 AD when the temple was destroyed there was no Temple to celebrate over concerning it's cleansing. So there arose a tradition about the lights of the Menorah in the Temple. Tradition says that in 165 BC when the temple was cleansed there was "only one flagon of oil, sealed with the signet of the high-priest, was found to feed the lamps. This, then, was *pure* oil, but the supply was barely sufficient for one day, lo, by a miracle, the oil increased, and the flagon remained filled for eight days, in memory of which it was ordered to illuminate for the same space of time the Temple and private houses" (5). The Menorah burned for 8 days! It burned until more oil could be consecrated *thus the 8 days of Chanukah.* So Chanukah occurs for eight days and is celebrated with lights, gifts and great joy.

"After the occupiers had been driven from the Temple, the Maccabees discovered that almost all of the ritual olive oil had been profaned. They found only a single container that was still sealed by the High Priest, with enough oil to keep the Menorah in the Temple lit for a single day. They used this, and miraculously, that oil burned for eight days (the time it took to have new oil pressed and made ready)" (6).

From the hesitating language of Josephus (Antiq. xii. 7, 7), we infer that the real origin of the practice of illuminating the Temple was unknown. A learned Jewish writer, Dr. Herzfeld, suggests, that to commemorate the descent of fire from heaven upon the altar in the Temple of Solomon (2 Chron 7:1), 'the Feast of Lights' was instituted when the sacred fire was relit on the purified altar of the second Temple (7).

So the congregation of Israel decreed that the rededication of the altar should be observed with joy and gladness at the same season each year, for eight days, beginning on the twenty-fifth of Kislev. The light of the Menorah is the symbol of the light of God. The fact that the light burned even when no supply was left is a perfect symbol of the eternity of God's Word. The heart of the celebration is not only the Rabbis retelling of the saga of revolt and renewal, but also the retelling of the divine experience of the Miracle of the Oil.

The Menorah

Chanukah is celebrated for eight consecutive days with the lighting of a candle for each day. The celebration centers around a nine-branch menorah. The Temple Menorah had seven branches but the Chanukah Menorah has nine branches, eight to remember the eight days of Hanukkah and one is the Shamus, the candle used to light the other candles.

By tradition the candles cannot be large enough to produce much light, as they must not be "working" candles. This created a problem. They could not light the celebration candles with another celebration candle. So, they added a ninth candle, called the "Shamash" (servant) candle, to light the celebration candles. Today, on most Chanukah Menorahs the Shamash candle is elevated above the other candles. Since when is a servant elevated above those he serves? How eloquently this pictures Him who came as a servant to become the superior light that alone can miraculously light the light of our life.

Jesus is that servant! He said: *"I speak that which I have seen with my father.."* (John 8: 18a). It was God who said to Moses: *"I will raise them up a Prophet from among their brethren, like unto thee, and will put my words in his mouth; and he shall speak unto them all that I shall command him."* (Deut. 18:18). Jesus also stated: *"For I came down from heaven, not to do mine own will, but* the *will of him that sent me."* (John 6:38). He is the fulfillment of Isaiah 53: 4, 5.

There was a disagreement between two rabbinical schools of thought - Hillel and the House of Shammai - on the proper way to light Hanukkah candles. Shammai said that eight candles should be lit from the start, and reduced by one candle every night, whereas Hillel argued in favor of starting with one candle and lighting an additional one every night. The custom today is based on Hillel's opinion

The Messiah in Chanukah

The law did not require Jews to be at the Temple in Jerusalem, as this was not one of the pilgrimage festivals. Every one observed it in his own place, not as a holy time. Jesus was there that He might improve those eight days of holiday for good purposes. Jesus walked in the temple in Solomon's porch when the Sadducees asked him *"How long will you keep us in suspense? If you are the Christ, tell us plainly" (John 10:24).* They pretended to want to know the truth, as if they were ready to embrace it; but it was not their intention. Jesus answered them, *"I did tell you, but you do not believe. The miracles I do in my Father's name speak for me, but you do not believe because you are not my sheep. My sheep listen to my voice; I know them, and they follow me. I give them eternal life, and they shall never perish; no one can snatch them out of my hand. My Father, who has given them to me, is greater than all; no one can snatch them out of my Father's hand. I and the Father are one" (John 10:25-30).* He had told them, and they believed not; why then should they be told again, merely to gratify their curiosity?

Chanukah's theme is of a miracle. During Chanukah Jesus spoke of His miracles: *"Do not believe me unless I do what my Father does. But if I do it, even though you do not believe me, believe the miracles, that you may know and understand that the Father is in me, and I in the Father" (John 10:37-38).* Jesus wanted the people of His day to see His miracles and believe in Him as a result. His miracles point to His divine and messianic identity. In this way Jesus personifies the message of Chanukah: God actively involved in the affairs of His people. Chanukah reminds us that God is a God of miracles, not just of concept and religious ideals. He has broken through into human history and continues to do so today.

Jesus preached three sermons in which he declared Himself the *"light of the world,"* and all three could have been during Chanukah, the Festival of Lights. (It is not clear from the text when this incident happened, but it was some time between the Feast of Tabernacles and the Feast of Dedication (Chanukah); both of these celebrations focused on light). *"Is it not written in your Law, 'I have said you are gods'? If he called them 'gods,' to whom the word of God came — and the Scripture cannot be broken — what about the one whom the Father set apart as his very own and sent into the world? Why then do you accuse me of blasphemy because I said, 'I am God's Son' (John 12:35-36)?*

Just before Jesus announced that He was the Light of the world, Jesus had shone upon the conscience of those who accused the adulteress in John 8. John also records Jesus healing a blind man (9:1-12) at about the same time (8:12 and 9:5) that Jesus declared himself to be the Light of the world. *When he had thus spoken, he spat on the ground, and made clay of the spittle, and he anointed the eyes of the blind man with the clay, And said unto him, Go, wash in the pool of Siloam, He went his way therefore, and washed, and came seeing (John 9:5-7).*

Many believe that our Messiah, the "light of the world," was conceived on the festival of lights - Chanukah. The Bible does not specifically say the date of Jesus' birth. It was not during the winter months because the sheep were in the pasture (Luke 2:8). A study of the time of the conception of John the Baptist reveals he was conceived about Sivan 30, the eleventh week (Luke 1:8-13, 24). Adding forty weeks, for a normal pregnancy reveals that John the Baptist was born on or about Passover (Nisan 14). Six months after John's conception, Mary conceived Jesus (Luke 1:26-33); therefore Jesus would have been conceived six months after Sivan 30 in the month of Kislev - Chanukah. Was the "light of the world," conceived on the Festival of Lights? Starting at Chanukah, which begins on Kislev 25 and continues for eight days, and counting through the nine months of Mary's pregnancy, one arrives at the approximate time of the birth of Jesus at the Festival of Tabernacles.

Footnotes for Chapter Seven

1- Michael Strassfeld. *The Jewish Holidays, A Guide & Commentary*. p. 162

2- Flavius Josephus. *Antiquities of the Jews*. Book 12, Chapter 5

3- Victor Buksbazen. *The Gospel in the Feasts of Israel*. p. 50.

4- - Nosson Scherman and Meir Zlotowitz. *Chanukah.* p. 56.

5- Alfred Edersheim. *The Temple.* p. 215.

6-The miracle of Hanukkah is described in the Talmud. *The Gemara,* in tractate *Shabbat 21b*

7- Alfred Edershiem. *The Temple.* p. 216.

Chapter Eight – Christmas
December 25

In those days Caesar Augustus issued a decree that a census should be taken of the entire Roman world. (This was the first census that took place while Quirinius was governor of Syria.) And everyone went to his own town to register. So Joseph also went up from the town of Nazareth in Galilee to Judea, to Bethlehem the town of David. He went there to register with Mary, who was pledged to be married to him and was expecting a child. While they were there, the time came for the baby to be born and she gave birth to her firstborn, a son. She wrapped him in cloths and placed him in a manger, because there was no room for them in the inn.

And there were shepherds living out in the fields nearby, keeping watch over their flocks at night. An angel of the Lord appeared to them, and the glory of the Lord shone around them, and they were terrified. But the angel said to them, "Do not be afraid. I bring you good news of great joy that will be for all the people. Today in the town of David a Savior has been born to you; he is Christ the Lord. This will be a sign to you: You will find a baby wrapped in cloths and lying in a manger." Suddenly a great company of the heavenly host appeared with the angel, praising God and saying, "Glory to God in the highest, and on earth peace to men on whom his favor rests."

When the angels had left them and gone into heaven, the shepherds said to one another, "Let's go to Bethlehem and see this thing that has happened, which the Lord has told us about." So they hurried off and found Mary and Joseph, and the baby, who was lying in the manger. When they had seen him, they spread the word concerning what had been told them about this child, and all who heard it were amazed at what the shepherds said to them. But Mary treasured up all these things and pondered them in her heart. The shepherds returned, glorifying and praising God for all the things they had heard and seen, which were just as they had been told. (Luke 2:1-20)

This is how the birth of Jesus Christ came about: His mother Mary was pledged to be married to Joseph, but before they came together, she was found to be with child through the Holy Spirit. Because Joseph her husband was a righteous man and did not want to expose her to public disgrace, he had in mind to divorce her quietly. But after he had considered this, an angel of the Lord appeared to him in a dream and said, "Joseph son of David, do not be afraid to take Mary home as your wife, because what is conceived in her is from the Holy Spirit. She will give birth to a son, and you are to give him the name Jesus, because he will save his people from their sins." All this took place to fulfill what the Lord had said through the prophet: "The virgin will be with child and will give birth to a son, and they will call him Immanuel" - which means, "God with us." When Joseph woke up, he did what the angel of the Lord had commanded him and took Mary home as his wife. But he had no union with her until she gave birth to a son. And he gave him the name Jesus.

After Jesus was born in Bethlehem in Judea, during the time of King Herod, Magi from the east came to Jerusalem and asked, "Where is the one who has been born king of the Jews? We saw his star in the east and have come to worship him." When King

Herod heard this he was disturbed, and all Jerusalem with him. When he had called together all the people's chief priests and teachers of the law, he asked them where the Christ was to be born. "In Bethlehem in Judea," they replied, "for this is what the prophet has written. "But you, Bethlehem, in the land of Judah, are be no means least among the rulers of Judah; for out of you will come a ruler who will be the shepherd of my people Israel." Then Herod called the Magi secretly and found out from them the exact time the star had appeared. He sent them to Bethlehem and said, "Go and make a careful search for the child. As soon as you find him, report to me, so that I too may go and worship him."

After they had heard the King, they went on their way, and the star they had seen in the east went ahead of them until it stopped over the place where the child was. Then, when they saw the star, they were overjoyed. On coming to the house, they saw the child with his mother Mary, and they bowed down and worshiped him. Then they opened their treasures and presented him with gifts of gold and of incense and of myrrh. And having been warned in a dream not to go back to Herod, they returned to their country by another route.

When they had gone, an angel of the Lord appeared to Joseph in a dream. "Get up," he said, "take the child and his mother and escape to Egypt. Stay there until I tell you, for Herod is going to search for the child to kill him." So he got up, took the child and his mother during the night and left for Egypt where he stayed until the death of Herod. And so was fulfilled what the Lord had said through the prophet: "Out of Egypt I called my son."

When Herod realized that the Magi had outwitted him, he was furious, and he gave orders to kill all the boys in Bethlehem and its vicinity who were two years old and under, in accordance with the time he had learned from the Magi. Then what was said through the prophet Jeremiah was fulfilled: "A voice is heard in Ramah, weeping and great mourning, Rachel weeping for her children and refusing to be comforted, because they are no more."

After Herod died, an angel of the Lord appeared in a dream to Joseph in Egypt and said, "Get up, take the child and his mother and go to the land of Israel, for those who were trying to take the child's life are dead." So he got up, took the child and his mother and went to the land of Israel. But when he heard that Archelaus as reigning in Judea in place of his father Herod, he was afraid to go there. Having been warned in a dream, he withdrew to the district of Galilee, and he went and lived in a town called Nazareth. So was fulfilled what was said through the prophets "He will be called a Nazarene." (Matthew 1: 19-2:23)

"There are no probabilities whatever that our Savior Jesus Christ was born on that day, and the observance of it is purely of traditional origin. However, I wish there were ten or a dozen Christmas-days in the year; for there is work enough in the world, and a little more rest would not hurt laboring people." - C.H. Spurgeon

I love Christmas because it is the celebration of a new beginning. Galatians

4:4-7 says - *fullness of the time, God sent his Son,* and it was a new beginning. That New beginning is experienced in every heart that receives Christ as their Savior. But of course, Christmas is attacked by many people as simply a re-making of a pagan holiday. But this is not true – it has always, only been about Jesus!

The Bible only has one story and that is the story of Redemption. All parts of Bible tell the same story of redemption. The story of the Church, the prophets, and even Feasts and Festivals of Israel - *everything* in the Bible tells the Redemption Story. And Christmas tells the story of redemption as well.

Now the celebration of the birth of Christ has become the most obvious religious-based public festival of American life. Its arrival in December is prepared for months in advance. It is the one event which generates the most anticipation and to which the most tradition and custom have attached themselves. Individual homes and whole cities dress up for Christmas. In popular sentiment it has eclipsed the greater feast of the Resurrection, and has completely dwarfed its twin festival, the Epiphany. But how did we get a feast of Christmas? What was its original purpose? How does it actually fit into the life of the Christian Church?

When it comes to the Christmas holiday, most people enjoy it so much they do not think about its meaning in deeper theological ways. It's kind of a very sentimental, "feel good" holiday that all enjoy - Christian or otherwise. Clergy, scholars, theologians, etc. look into the deeper issues but even they usually end up discussing the Regulative Principle of Scripture – whether or not we should celebrate Christmas based on our view of what Scripture allows. Throughout the centuries historians, theologians and others argued the merit of Christmas and its significance to Christianity. Atheists, Agnostics and people of non-Christian faiths love to show all the inconsistencies between what the Bible says about the birth of Jesus and what we say about it in the church today and declare that Christianity therefore is a false religion.

Now it is true that no one can ever establish the date of Christ's birth or the origin of the festival without any doubt. However this is not necessary in order for us to have a Christ centered, life refreshing celebration of the birth of the one who came to give us salvation and eternal life.

It does seem that, in today's world, no one takes Christmas very seriously especially because of all the commercialism, materialism and paganism that seems to accompany it. However the perversion of the celebration does not mean that it has no value in its true meaning. In the mind of the ancient church Christmas was a necessary celebration because it is the beginning of the story of our redemption. The birth of Christ leads to the ministry and death of Christ which in turn leads to the resurrection of Christ which in turn leads to His second coming at the end of time. It is necessary to begin the story of the resurrection by reminding us that Jesus was born into this world as a human baby taking a human nature in addition to His divine nature.

In other words, Christmas does not have to be a secular or despised holiday. It was intended by the early church to be part of the story of redemption. The Christian Calendar begins with the birth of Christ, because the church itself begins with Christ.

The Lord Jesus Christ created the church, He died for the church, He redeemed the church, He is the King and Head of the church today and, He is coming back for His church. Christmas can be a wonderful season of worship to our Lord and God if we will give it back its true significance.

Origin of the Word "Christmas"

The word for Christmas in late Old English is *Cristes Maesse*, the Mass of Christ, first found in 1038, and *Cristes-messe*, in 1131. In Dutch it is *Kerst-misse*, in Latin *Dies Natalis*, whence comes the French *Noël*, and Italian *Il natale*; in German *Weihnachtsfest*, from the preceding sacred vigil. The feast was not originally called Christmas or Nativity in the early church, but rather Epiphany or "Manifestation." It celebrated the idea of Christ's coming and manifesting Himself through several events in the New Testament and in the East this feast of "coming" was generally kept on January 6th and in the West on December 25th (1).

The History of Christmas

Now, the Bible never commanded us to celebrate the birth of Christ just as it never commanded the Jews to celebrate Purim or Chanukah. No historical evidence has ever been found that support the celebration of Christ's birth during the apostolic or early post-apostolic era. Regarding the attitude of early Christians toward such things, Auld says--"As for the first believers, they had NOT THE SLIGHTEST INTEREST IN ANYTHING OF THE KIND. Hope in the Lord's imminent return from heaven in great power and glory was the flame that fired their devotion" (2).

The Christian Church in the first three centuries of its existence knew of only one great festival, Pentecost. However, what the early church meant by Pentecost was the complete celebration of the Christian Passover from the cross and resurrection to the 50th day commemorating the descent of the Holy Spirit. Every Sunday was considered a feast in that it was a gathering to proclaim the mighty redemption brought by the death and resurrection of Christ.

In time the celebration of martyrs' days, that is, the yearly anniversary of a martyr's death came to be celebrated. But these festivals were local and usually conducted at the martyr's tomb. It is not until the fourth century that the idea of celebrating occasions in the earthly life of our Lord started to become popular. Much of this is due to the Church of Jerusalem. Special celebrations, which were devised on the actual or supposed sites of the events of the life of Christ, lent themselves particularly well to the celebration of historical remembrances. So interest developed in where Jesus was born, where He grew up, where He performed miracles, etc. It is to the Church of Rome, that we must give the credit for the origins of the feast of the birth of Christ. But on what was this feast based and why was December 25th chosen as the day for its celebration (3)?

Christmas was not among the earliest festivals of the Church. Irenaeus and Tertullian omit it from their lists of feasts. The first confirmation of the feast of the Nativity was found in Alexandria, Egypt; about 200 AD. Clement of Alexandria first reported the feast and the first evidence of the feast is from Egypt. In 200 AD, Clement says that certain Egyptian theologians "over curiously" assign, not the year alone, but the day of Christ's birth, placing it on 25 Pachon (20 May) in the twenty-eighth year of

Augustus (though they did this believing that the ninth month, in which Christ was born, was the ninth of their own calendar). Sadly, scholars have shown that there is no month in the year to which respectable authorities have not assigned Christ's birth down through history. But this is our earliest record of the feast of the nativity (4).

The earliest literary evidence we have of a date for a celebration of the Nativity of Christ is in the Roman *Chronograph* of Furius Dionysius Philocalus - sometimes called the *Philocalian Calendar* - written between 336 and 354 AD. Philocalus was a Christian interested in chronological information. His document consists of two chronological lists. The first is a list of the consuls of Rome thus indicating a year; the second, entitled *Depositio Martyrum,* indicates death dates (and so memorial dates) of the more famous Christian martyrs and saints. Among those listed are: Saints Peter and Paul (29th June), St Sylvester (31st December) and African martyrs Saints Perpetua and Felicity (7th March) as well as St Cyprian (16th September). But also included is the Chair of Peter (22nd February). And at the head of this list is an entry: VIII Kal. Ian. Natus Christus in Bethleem Iudeae ("on the eighth day before the Kalends of January {= 25th December} Christ was born in Bethlehem of Judea"). This suggests that Christmas was marked as a feast among Christians at Rome between 336 and 354 (5).

The feast of Alexandria was not today's Christmas. The feast was known as Epiphany (from the Greek epi and phainein meaning to show or shine upon). Epiphany was the celebration of Christ's' manifestation. It did not originally concentrate exclusively on the birth of our Lord, but celebrated several aspects of His manifestation: the Annunciation (visit of the Angel Gabriel), the Birth in the stable, the Acknowledgment of Christ's divinity (the visit and adoration of the Magi), the Theophany (Christ's baptism in the Jordan), and the First Miracle at Cana in Galilee. All of these themes came in one way or another to be associated with the feast of the Epiphany. In the Greek Orthodox Church the Sanctification of the Waters is a large part of the Epiphany celebrations in remembrance of Christ's baptism and the manifestation of the Trinity (6).

Clement of Alexandria put the Annunciation on May 20, the Acknowledgment of Christ's Divinity on January 6, and the Theophany on November 6. The church of Alexandria celebrated the Epiphany from January 6-10. Hippolytus of Rome also fixed Christ birth on December 25 in 212 A.D. He believed that Jesus' life from annunciation to crucifixion was precisely thirty-three years and that both events occurred on March 25. By calculating nine months from the annunciation he arrived at December 25 as Christ's birth. The ambiguity of all the data however, discredits these calculations.

Pope Liberius I started Epiphany in the Roman Church sometime in 355-357 AD. In 357 Liberius' sermon on the feast was more appropriate to the Epiphany than Christmas. Later St. Augustine also established the feast of Christmas in December however he supported and practiced the holy celebration of both days. He placed Christmas on December 25 and Epiphany on January 6and he says "Let us, therefore, with the joy of the Spirit, hold dear these two days, the Nativity and the Manifestation of our Lord." (7).

By the end of the forth century every western calendar assigned Christ's birth on December 25. De Santi, a monk from the Eastern Church, argues that Roman Christians took over the Eastern Epiphany and made a new feast. Later East and West divided their feast. Western churches celebrated Christmas on December 25 and Eastern Churches kept the Epiphany on January 6. Even today the Eastern Orthodox Church celebrates Epiphany on January 6.

In Constantinople Christmas appears to have been introduced in 379 or 380. In 383 A.D. Churches in Cyprus, Mesopotamia, Armenia, and Asia Minor started celebrating Epiphany. The Church of Cyprus was celebrating Christ's birth on December 25 before 380 A.D. The church of Cyprus separated Christ's birth from Epiphany and celebrated Christ's birth on December 25 and Epiphany on January 6. In 385, Silvia of Bordeaux in Jerusalem separated Christ's birth from Epiphany and started to celebrate Christ's birth on December 25. From a sermon of St. John Chrysostom, at the time a renowned ascetic and preacher in his native Antioch, it appears that the feast was first celebrated there on December 25, 386.

Once this double feast, Christmas-Epiphany, entered the life of the Church it became, like Easter-Pentecost, an occasion for the celebration of baptism. The feast of Christ's coming was seen to be appropriate for the administration of the sacrament by which Christ would come to the new believer. From these centers it spread throughout the Christian East, being adopted in Alexandria around 432 and in Jerusalem a century or more later. The Armenians, alone among ancient Christian churches, have never adopted it, and to this day celebrate Christ's birth, manifestation to the magi, and baptism are celebrated on January 6th (8).

Western churches, in turn, gradually adopted the January 6th Epiphany feast from the East, Rome doing so sometime between 366 and 394. But in the West, the feast was generally presented as the commemoration of the visit of the magi to the infant Christ, and as such, it was an important feast, but not one of the most important ones—a striking contrast to its position in the East, where it remains the second most important festival of the church year, second only to Easter.

In the East, Epiphany far outstrips Christmas. The reason is that the feast celebrates Christ's baptism in the Jordan and the occasion on which the Voice of the Father and the Descent of the Spirit both manifested for the first time to mortal men the divinity of the Incarnate Christ and the Trinity of the Persons in the One Godhead.

Pagan Roots a Mistake

The idea that the date of Christmas was taken from the pagans goes back to two scholars from the late seventeenth and early eighteenth centuries. Paul Ernst Jablonski, a German Protestant, wished to show that the celebration of Christ's birth on December 25th was one of the many "paganizations" of Christianity that the Church of the fourth century embraced, as one of many "degenerations" that transformed pure apostolic Christianity into Catholicism. Dom Jean Hardouin, a Benedictine monk, tried to show that the Catholic Church adopted pagan festivals for Christian purposes without paganizing the gospel.

In the Julian calendar, created in 45 B.C. under Julius Caesar, the winter solstice fell on December 25th, and it therefore seemed obvious to Jablonski and Hardouin that the day must have had a pagan significance before it had a Christian one. But in fact, the date had no religious significance in the Roman pagan festal calendar before Aurelian's time, nor did the cult of the sun play a prominent role in Rome before him.

There were two temples of the sun in Rome, one of which (maintained by the clan into which Aurelian was born or adopted) celebrated its dedication festival on August 9th, the other of which celebrated its dedication festival on August 28th. But both of these cults fell into neglect in the second century, when eastern cults of the sun, such as Mithraism, began to win a following in Rome. And in any case, none of these cults, old or new, had festivals associated with solstices or equinoxes.

As things actually happened, Aurelian, who ruled from 270 until his assassination in 275, was hostile to Christianity and appears to have promoted the establishment of the festival of the "Birth of the Unconquered Sun" as a device to unify the various pagan cults of the Roman Empire around a commemoration of the annual "rebirth" of the sun. He led an empire that appeared to be collapsing in the face of internal unrest, rebellions in the provinces, economic decay, and repeated attacks from German tribes to the north and the Persian Empire to the east.

In creating the new feast, he intended the beginning of the lengthening of the daylight, and the arresting of the lengthening of darkness, on December 25th to be a symbol of the hoped-for "rebirth," or perpetual rejuvenation, of the Roman Empire, resulting from the maintenance of the worship of the gods whose tutelage (the Romans thought) had brought Rome to greatness and world-rule. And if it happened to co-opt the Christian celebration, so much the better.

Thus, as Professor Tighe Associate Professor of History at Muhlenberg College says, "December 25th as the date of the Christ's birth appears to owe nothing whatsoever to pagan influences upon the practice of the Church during or after Constantine's time. It is wholly unlikely to have been the actual date of Christ's birth, but it arose entirely from the efforts of early Latin Christians to determine the historical date of Christ's death. And the pagan feast which the Emperor Aurelian instituted on that date in the year 274 was not only an effort to use the winter solstice to make a political statement, but also almost certainly an attempt to give a pagan significance to a date already of importance to Roman Christians. The Christians, in turn, could at a later date re-appropriate the pagan "Birth of the Unconquered Sun" to refer, on the occasion of the birth of Christ, to the rising of the "Sun of Salvation" or the "Sun of Justice"" (9).

According to Prof. Tighe, cultures have their most important holiday in winter because there is less agricultural work to do at this time. Examples of this holiday are Yule and Saturnalia. As mentioned above the pagan festival of the "Birth of the Unconquered Son" instituted by the Roman Emperor Aurelian on December 24, 274, was almost certainly an attempt to create a pagan alternative to a date that was already of some significance to Roman Christians.

Augustine (354 – 430) had to exhort the brethren not to solemnize the day on account of the sun like the heathen, but rather on account of Him who made the sun. Leo the Great (d. 461) rebuked those who thought that Christmas was observed for the solstice and not the nativity of Christ. Thus the "pagan origins of Christmas" is a myth without historical substance.

The Date of Christmas

The actual historical facts surrounding the birth of Christ are clouded in mystery. No one really knows when Jesus was born. Only certain facts can be deducted from the Biblical account and from history. For one thing, Jesus was definitely born in B.C. (Before Christ!). This is known because Herod the Great died in 4 B.C., and Herod figures in the account of the Nativity given by St. Matthew. Jesus was definitely not born in winter. St. Luke mentions that the shepherds were staying out in the pastureland with their flocks, an event that does not take place in winter. So we must look elsewhere for the origin of the late December celebration of the Nativity in the calendar of the church.

In ancient Judaism, as mentioned above, there was a common belief in the Integral Age, which is the belief that the prophets of Israel died on the on the same date as their birth or conception. The ancient Christians, it seems, inherited this belief to some extent (this may be behind the long-standing Christian custom of referring to the date of a martyr's death as their "birthday in heaven.").

According to ancient western calculations, Jesus was crucified on March 25, so they assumed that March 25 was the date of Jesus' conception. It is to this day, commemorated almost universally among Christians as the Feast of the Annunciation, when the Archangel Gabriel brought the good tidings of a savior to the Virgin Mary, who became incarnate in her womb. Nine months after March 25 leads to December 25, which would be the birthday of Jesus Christ if all those assumptions and calculations were correct. They aren't correct, but the fact remains that the date has a Christian origin.

Meanwhile, back in the east, Christians calculated the date of the crucifixion independently and came up with April 6. Nine months after April 6 is January 6. So the birth of Christ was celebrated on that day. December 25th is Christmas, and January 6th is Epiphany. Eventually, Christmas spread to the east and Epiphany spread to the west and the two days became differentiated. Today, Christmas is the celebration of the Nativity and the Epiphany is the celebration of Jesus' ministry to the Gentiles.

So we do not find the origin of the winter feast of the Nativity in the historical facts available concerning the birth of Christ. Where do we find it? Why did the Church pick Dec. 25th?

There are at least two main possibilities and the first one is found in understanding the Festival of Lights – Chanukah – and its dates as we saw in Chapter Seven on Chanukah. The Temple was cleansed and rededicated on Kislev 25, which corresponds roughly to our December 25th. In John 9-11 we are told that Jesus was at the Temple on the Feast of Dedication (Chanukah) and at that time He declares that He is the Light of the World.

After 70 AD when the temple was destroyed there was no temple to celebrate over its cleansing. So there arose a tradition about the lights, which said that after 165 BC the Temple was cleansed, but there was only one day of consecrated oil left and it took 8 days to make more. So they poured one jar into the Menorah and lit it then a miracle happened and it burned for 8 days until more oil could be consecrated - thus *the 8 days of Chanukah.* So when church wanted to celebrate Christmas they choose Kislev 25th which is the equivalent of Dec. 25th.

A Second Reason for choosing Dec. 25th was because of the timing of the birth of John the Baptist. John the Baptist father was Zechariah who was a Priest. There were so many Priests and Levites that King David had divided them into 12 courses. Each course served for 2 non-consecutive weeks of the year with the exception of the three pilgrim feasts when all the priests served together.

Zechariah was in the course of Abijah and we know that they served in the 8th course. The Jewish year begins on Nissan 1 (our March & April) and the first course of Priests would serve that week. The next week – the second course would serve. The third week was Passover when they would all serve. Then in the next week, the fourth week, the third course would serve and so on until the 8th week. This was when Zechariah would have served and this week was in the middle of June.

At this time Zechariah was told that he would have a son and soon after he returned home, his wife Elizabeth conceived. Six months later the Angel tells Mary she will conceive. She is also told about Elizabeth's pregnancy and goes to visit her. So this would be in December.

Now John is born 3 months later (March) around the time of Passover. This is interesting because the Jews – even to this day - look for the Elijah – the forerunner of the Messiah to come at Passover time. John the Baptist, the Elijah or forerunner of Jesus was born on or near the time of Passover just as the Jews were expecting!

This means then, that Jesus would have been born in the fall 6 months later in the month of Tishri, which is at the time of the feast of Tabernacles. If He was born on the first day of Tishri on the first day of the feast, then He world have been circumcised on the 8th day, which was the "great day of the feast" of Tabernacles. This is the time when the people pray for the blessings of God on their future.

Finally, the normal gestation period is 9 months and the ideal time for pregnancy is 278 days. 278 days backwards from September 29th is December 25th. Jesus was not born on Dec. 25th but He could have been conceived on Dec. 25th. After all, the true miracle was not His birth, which was a normal birth, but rather it was His conception that was supernatural!

So you can see that December 25th is about the celebration of the birth of Jesus Christ our Savior and always has been. In the fullness of time, God sent His Son into the world to redeem us from all unrighteousness and make us right with Him once again for all eternity!

Christmas Customs
Popular merry-making. The Church forbids, in 425, circus games on 25

December; though not till 529 is cessation of work imposed. The Second Council of Tours proclaims, in 566 or 567, the sanctity of the "twelve days" from Christmas to Epiphany, and the duty of the Advent fast. The Church eventually orders a universal communion, and in 563 forbids fasting on Christmas Day. Popular merry-making, however, so increased that the "Laws of King Canute" in 1110, order a fast from Christmas to Epiphany. (10)

The crib (crèche) or nativity scene. St. Francis of Assisi in 1223 originated the crib of today by laicizing (lay-a-sizing – letting the lay people do it) a hitherto Clergy custom, henceforward extra-liturgical and popular. The presence of ox and ass is due to a misinterpretation of Isaiah 1:3 and Habakkuk 3:2 ("Itala" version), though they appear in the unique fourth-century "Nativity" discovered in the St. Sebastian catacombs in 1877.

Hymns and carols. The degeneration of the mystery plays in part occasioned the diffusion of Noels, Pastorals, and Carols, to which was accorded, at times, a quasi-liturgical position. However, singing and caroling at Christmas is one of the oldest folk customs of the day and has been present since the time when Christianity and Christmas season were still at their budding stages. Originally, music compositions and songs at Christmas were in the form of chants and hymns. Caroling originally meant 'circle dance' and the words to accompany this festive dance were later added to the tradition.

In the fourth century, is the first hymn for the Nativity. Initially, the church looked down upon carols and carol singing as a pagan custom and they could not be included in the sacred services. However, in the countryside, many simple folk songs and Nativity carols were written and gained popularity too. Other hymns were written for Christmas in the eleventh and twelfth centuries, the earliest Noels from the eleventh, and the earliest Carols from the thirteenth. "Adeste Fideles" is, at the earliest, of the seventeenth century. These essentially popular airs, and even words, must, however, have existed long before they were put down in writing.

In 1223, Saint Francis of Assisi introduced carols into the formal worship of the church during a Christmas Midnight Mass in a cave in Greccio, in the province of Umbria. That night, the songs and music that accompanied this sacred and formal event were not hymns but carols. Ever since then, carols caught on with the masses and were at their prime in the Middle Ages, when they were almost always a part of the mystery plays.

There was a time, when wandering minstrels and waits or watchmen that guarded the old walled cities in the night used to pass their time by singing carols and also sang them to the people who used to pass them by. They would go from home to home, singing carols and entertaining people and maybe get a treat in return. Later groups of musicians began singing carols and playing them for various events that were held during the Christmas season.

Greenery. Gervase of Tilbury (thirteen century) says that in England grain is exposed on Christmas night to gain fertility from the dew, which falls that night; the tradition that trees and flowers blossomed on this night is first quoted from an Arab geographer of the tenth century, and extended to England. In a thirteenth-century French epic, candles are seen on the flowering tree. In England it was Joseph of Arimathea's rod, which flowered at Glastonbury and elsewhere; when September 3 became September 14, in 1752, 2000 people watched to see if the Quainton thorn (cratagus præcox) would blow on Christmas New Style; and as it did not, they refused to keep the New Style festival. From this belief of the calends practice of greenery decorations (forbidden by Archbishop Martin of Braga, c. 575, mistletoe was bequeathed by the Druids) developed the Christmas tree, first definitely mentioned in 1605 at Strasburg, and introduced into France and England in 1840 only by Princess Helena of Mecklenburg and the Prince Consort respectively.

The Mysterious Visitor. Only with great caution should the mysterious benefactor of Christmas night -- Knecht Ruprecht, Pelzmärtel on a wooden horse, St. Martin on a white charger, St. Nicholas and his "reformed" equivalent, Father Christmas be used in the Christmas celebrations. Knecht Ruprecht, at any rate (first found in a mystery of 1668 and condemned in 1680 as a devil) was only a servant of the Holy Child. Holiday Trivia - St. Nicholas who was the Bishop of Myra and was at the Council of Nicea when they picked the date to celebrate Easter. He did not help to pick the date of Christmas and as far as we know never had anything to do with Christmas while he was alive!

Conclusion

The Church at one time conquered and transformed that pagan holiday into the sublime celebration of the coming of the Sun of Righteousness. She still is challenged to transform and transfigure and to proclaim that coming and to lead men beyond tinsel and cheap lights to the true meaning of this holiday: the glorification of the true Gladsome Light of the Holy Glory of the Immortal Father, heavenly, holy, blessed Jesus Christ our Lord (11)!

Footnotes for Chapter 8

1- www.newadvent.org/cathen/03724b.htm

2- http://www.antipas.org/books/xmas/xmas4.html

3- Antony Bassoline. Word Magazine, December 1979. pp. 5-6

4- F.L. Cross and E.A. Livingstone, Editors. The Oxford Dictionary of The Christian Church. p. 280.

5- Ibid. p. 1084.

6- Marguerite Ickis. *The Book of Religious Holidays and Celebrations.* p. 105.

7- Thomas Lawler. *St Augustine: Sermons for Christmas and Epiphany.* p. 8.

8- Earl and Alice Count. 4000 Years of Christmas. p. 43.

9 – William J. Tighe. Touchstone magazine. December, 2003.

10- Conor McCarthy. Love, Sex and marriage in the middle Ages. p. 102.

11- Antony Bassoline. *Word Magazine*. December 1979, pp. 5-6.

Appendixes

Appendix One
A Typical Sabbath Day

At about 2 or 3pm on Friday afternoon, observant Jews leave the office to begin Sabbath preparations. The mood is much like preparing for the arrival of a special, beloved guest: the house is cleaned, the family bathes and dresses up, the best dishes and tableware are set, a festive meal is prepared. In addition, everything that cannot be done during Sabbath must be set up in advance: lights and appliances must be set (or timers placed on them, if the household does so), the light bulb in the refrigerator must be removed or unscrewed, so it does not turn on when you open it, and preparations for the remaining Sabbath meals must be made.

The Sabbath, like all Jewish days, begins at sunset, because in the story of creation in Genesis Ch. 1. From this, we infer that a day begins with evening, that is, sunset. For the precise time when Sabbath begins and ends in your area, consult the list of candle lighting times provided by the Orthodox Union, by Chabad or by any Jewish calendar. In ancient Jerusalem a priest would ascend to the top of the Tower of Light, which was situated, on the northwestern hill of the Tyropean Valley in the city and watch the sun set. As soon as it went below the horizon he would send a signal to another priest standing at the southwest tower of the temple where he would blow a horn that would inform all the people that the Sabbath had begun. At the end of the Sabbath the process would be repeated.

Sabbath candles are lit and a blessing is recited no later than eighteen minutes before sunset. This ritual, performed by the woman of the house, officially marks the beginning of the Sabbath. Two candles are lit, representing the two commandments: remember and observe, discussed above. The family then attends a brief evening service (about 45 minutes).

After services, the family comes home for a festive, leisurely dinner. Before dinner, the man of the house recites Kiddush, a prayer over wine sanctifying the Sabbath. The usual prayer for eating bread is recited over two loaves of "challah", a sweet, eggy bread shaped in a braid. The family then eats dinner. Although there are no specific requirements or customs regarding what to eat, meals are generally stewed or slow cooked items, because of the prohibition against cooking during Sabbath. (Things that are mostly cooked before Sabbath and then reheated or kept warm are OK).

After dinner, the grace after meals is recited. Although this is done every day, on Sabbath, it is done in a leisurely manner with many upbeat tunes. By the time all of this is completed, it may be 9PM or later. The family has an hour or two to talk or study Torah, and then go to sleep.

The next morning Sabbath services begin around 9AM and continue until about noon. After services, the family says Kiddush again and has another leisurely, festive meal. A typical afternoon meal is a very slowly cooked stew. By the time grace after meals is done, it is about 2PM. The family studies Torah for a while, talks, takes an afternoon walk, plays some checkers, or engages in other leisure activities. A short afternoon nap is not uncommon. It is traditional to have a third meal before Sabbath is over. This is usually a light meal in the late afternoon.

The Sabbath ends at nightfall, when three stars are visible, approximately 40 minutes after sunset. At the conclusion of the Sabbath, the family performs a concluding ritual called Havdalah (separation, division). Blessings are recited over wine, spices and candles. Then a blessing is recited regarding the division between the sacred and the secular, between the Sabbath and the working days, etc. As you can see, the Sabbath is a very full day when it is properly observed, and very relaxing.

Appendix Two

Appendix Three - The Easter Praise of Christ
Saint Melito of Sardis, bishop
Early Church Father

This selection comes from a Resurrection homily from one of the greatest 2nd century Church Fathers, Melito of Sardis. Though Melito's writings were extremely popular, this wonderful Paschal homily was lost until the 20th century. This is the oldest known homily on the resurrection of Jesus.

We should understand, beloved, that the paschal mystery is at once old and new, transitory and eternal, corruptible and incorruptible, mortal and immortal. In terms of the Law it is old, in terms of the Word it is new. In its figure it is passing, in its grace it is eternal. It is corruptible in the sacrifice of the lamb, incorruptible in the eternal life of the Lord. It is mortal in his burial in the earth, immortal in his resurrection from the dead

The Law indeed is old, but the Word is new. The type is transitory, but grace is eternal. The lamb was corruptible, but the Lord is incorruptible. He was slain as a lamb; he rose again as God. *He was led like a sheep to the slaughter,* yet he was not a sheep. He was silent as a lamb, yet he was not a lamb. The type has passed away; the reality has come. The lamb gives place to God, the sheep gives place to a man, and the man is Christ, who fills the whole of creation. The sacrifice of the lamb, the celebration of the Passover, and the prescriptions of the Law have been fulfilled in Jesus Christ. Under the old Law, and still more under the new dispensation, everything pointed toward him.

Both the Law and the Word came forth from Zion and Jerusalem, but now the Law has given place to the Word, the old to the new. The commandment has become grace, the type a reality. The lamb has become a Son, the sheep a man, and man, God.

The Lord, though he was God, became man. He suffered for the sake of those who suffer, he was bound for those in bonds, condemned for the guilty, buried for those who lie in the grave; but he rose from the dead, and cried aloud: *Who will contend with me? Let him confront me.* I have freed the condemned, brought the dead back to life, raised men from their graves. Who has anything to say against me? I, he said, am the Christ; I have destroyed death, triumphed over the enemy, trampled hell underfoot, bound the strong one, and taken men up to the heights of heaven: I am the Christ.

Come, then, all you nations of men, receive forgiveness for the sins that defile you. I am your forgiveness. I am the Passover that brings salvation. I am the lamb who was immolated for you. I am your ransom, your life, your resurrection, your light; I am your salvation and your king. I will bring you to the heights of heaven. With my own right hand I will raise you up, and I will show you the eternal Father.

Appendix Four
The Full Easter Season Schedule

Below is the Easter Season schedule in both the Eastern and Western Christian Churches combined. Most Protestant Churches do not follow these events at all. However, many Protestant traditions come from this schedule and the events contained in it.

Pre-Lent Season
    Before Great Lent, there is a five-week Pre-Lent season, to prepare for Lent. The Sundays in this season are:

Zachaeus Sunday
Publiccan and Pharisee Sunday
Prodigal Son Sunday
Meatfare Sunday

Meatfare Sunday (*Sunday of the Last Judgment*), the last day to eat meat before Easter.

On this day the Eastern Churches commemorate the inescapable second coming of Christ, ("ordained by the most divine Fathers to be observed after the second parable of the Prodigal"), so that no one who has learned of the love of God for mankind will live in laziness saying, "God loves mankind, and when I am separated from Him by sin, all is prepared for my restoration" (6).

Cheesefare Sunday

Cheesefare Sunday (*Sunday of Forgiveness*), the last day to eat dairy products before Easter; on this Sunday, Eastern Christians identify with Adam and Eve, and forgive each other in order to obtain forgiveness from God, typically in a Forgiveness Vespers service that Sunday evening. It is during Forgiveness Vespers that the decor of the church is changed to reflect a repentant mood. The Service culminates with the Ceremony of Mutual Forgiveness, at which all present will bow down before one another and ask forgiveness. In this way, the faithful begin Lent with a clean conscience, with forgiveness, and with renewed Christian love.

Great Lent

This is the greatest fasting period in the church year in Eastern Christianity, which prepares Christians for the greatest feast of the church year, Easter. Although it is in many ways similar to Lent in Western Christianity, there are several important differences in the timing of Lent (besides the way the date of Easter is calculated), the underlying theology, and how it is practiced, both liturgically in the church and personally.

Clean Monday

The common term for this day, "Clean Monday," refers to the leaving behind of sinful attitudes and non-fasting foods.

Liturgically speaking, Clean Monday - and thus Lent itself - begins on the Sunday night before Lent, at a special service called Forgiveness Vespers (see above). The entire first week of Great Lent is often referred to as "Clean Week," and it is customary to go to Confession during this week, and to clean your house thoroughly.

84

Shrove Monday
> The word *shrove* means to obtain absolution for one's sins by confessing and doing penance. Shrove Monday is the Monday before Ash Wednesday.

Shrove Tuesday
> Shrove Tuesday gets its name from the "shriving" (confession) that Anglo-Saxon Christians were expected to give immediately before Lent.
>
> > Shrove Tuesday is the last day of "shrovetide," which is the English equivalent to the Carnival tradition that developed separately out of the countries of Latin Europe. In countries of the Carnival tradition, the day before Ash Wednesday is known either as the "Tuesday of Carnival" or "Fat Tuesday" The term "Shrove Tuesday" is not widely known in the United States, especially in those regions that celebrate Mardi Gras on the day before Ash Wednesday.

Ash Wednesday
> In the Western Christian calendar, Ash Wednesday is the first day of Lent and occurs forty-six days before Easter. As the first day of Lent, it comes the day after Mardi Gras (Fat Tuesday), the last day of the Carnival season. According to the Oxford English Dictionary, the word "Carnival" is derived from Latin *carnem levare* (removal of the meat) or *carnem laxare* (leaving the meat).
>
> At services of worship on this day, ashes are imposed on the foreheads of the faithful. The priest, minister, or in some cases officiating layperson marks the forehead of each participant with black ashes, in the shape of a cross, which the worshiper traditionally retains until washing it off after sundown. The symbolism echoes the ancient Near Eastern tradition of throwing ash over one's head signifying repentance before God. The priest or minister offers the worshiper an instruction while applying the ashes.
>
> Ash Wednesday is a time for repentance. Ashes were used in ancient times, according to the Bible, to express penitence. Dusting themselves with ashes was the penitent's way of expressing sorrow for sins and faults. An ancient example of one expressing his penitence is found in Job 42:3-6. Job says to God: *"I have heard of thee by the hearing of the ear: but now mine eye seeth thee. Wherefore I abhor myself, and repent in dust and ashes*
>
> However, some Christians, who do not celebrate Ash Wednesday, say that the practice is not consistent with Scripture and is of pagan origin. They usually cite Matthew 6:16–18, where Jesus gave prescriptions for fasting: "*And whenever you fast, do not look dismal, like the hypocrites, for they disfigure their faces so as to show others that they are fasting. Truly I tell you, they have received their reward. But when you fast, put oil on your head and wash your face, so that your fasting may be seen not by others but by your Father who is in secret; and your Father who sees in secret will reward you.*" These groups argue that Jesus warned against fasting to gain favor from other people and that he also warned his followers that they should fast in private, not letting others know they were

fasting. For these reasons, some Christian denominations do not endorse the practice. Others, however, point out that this very passage from Matthew is the one, not coincidentally, appointed to be read on Ash Wednesday.

40 Days of Lent

The forty-day period is symbolic of the 40 days spent by Jesus in the wilderness. The number forty has many other Biblical significances: the forty days Moses spent on Mount Sinai with God; the forty days and nights Elijah spent walking to Mt. Horeb; God makes it rain for forty days and forty nights in the story of Noah; the Hebrew people wandered forty years traveling to the Promised Land; Jonah in his prophecy of judgment gave the city of Nineveh forty days grace in which to repent. And of course the Temptation of Jesus in the wilderness laster 40 days. The Lenten period of forty days owes its origin to the Latin word *quadragesima*, referring to the forty hours of total fast that preceded the Easter celebration in the early Church. Lent is actually longer than 40 days, but since Sunday is always considered a feast day, only week days are counted.

Lazarus Saturday

Lazarus Saturday is the day before Palm Sunday, and is liturgically linked to it. The feast celebrates the resurrection of Lazarus in John 11:1-45.

Lazarus Saturday and Palm Sunday together hold a unique position in the church year, as days of joy and triumph interposed between the penitence of Great Lent and the mourning of Holy Week.

The week before Easter is very special in the Christian tradition and begins with:

Palm Sunday

Before entering Jerusalem, Jesus was staying at Bethany with Lazarus, and his sisters Mary and Martha. While there, Jesus sent two unnamed disciples to the village over against them, in order to retrieve a colt that had been tied up but never been ridden, and to say, if questioned, that the colt was needed by the Lord but would be returned in a short period of time. Then Jesus then rode the colt into Jerusalem, after the disciples had first put their cloaks on it, so as to make it more comfortable. The Gospels go on to describe how Jesus rode into Jerusalem, and how the people there lay down their cloaks in front of him, and also lay down small branches of trees. The people are also described as singing part of Psalm 118 - ...*Blessed is he who comes in the name of the Lord. Blessed is the coming kingdom of our father, David. ...* (18:25-26). Where this entry is supposed to have taken place is unspecified; some scholars argue that the Golden Gate is the likely location, since that was where it was believed the Jewish messiah would enter Jerusalem; other scholars think that an entrance to the south, which had stairs leading directly to the Temple, would be more likely.

Holy Wednesday or Spy Wednesday

In Western Christianity, *Holy Wednesday* is widely known as *Spy Wednesday*, as being the day that Judas Iscariot first conspired with the Sanhedrin to betray Jesus for thirty silver coins

According to Jewish tradition this day is the *Fast of the First Born Sons*. It is the day when the Jews mourn the death of the first born sons of the Egyptians at the time of the Exodus. This is because God does not allow His people to rejoice in the death of their enemies. It is also a time to worship God with praise and thanksgiving for *"passing over"* their homes in Egypt and saving their first born sons. This day was observed by everyone staying in their homes and worshipping the Lord as a family.

Because of this the Church has often called this day *"Silent Wednesday"* because the Scriptures do not record Jesus doing anything on this day. He did not do anything on this day because as a faithful Jew he stayed home with Mary, Martha and Lazarus and overused the *Fast of the First Born Sons*.

Maundy Thursday

In the Christian calendar, Maundy Thursday is the feast or holy day on the Thursday before Easter that commemorates the Last Supper of Jesus Christ with the Apostles. On this day four events are commemorated: the washing of the Disciples' feet by Jesus Christ, the institution of the Lord's Supper, the agony of Christ in the Garden of Gethsemane, and the betrayal of Christ by Judas Iscariot.

Good Friday

Good Friday is the Friday before Easter (Easter now always falls on a Sunday in the West). It commemorates the crucifixion and death of Jesus at Calvary.

Holy Saturday - Silent Saturday

Easter Vigil - The Easter Vigil, also called the Paschal Vigil or the Great Vigil of Easter, is a service held in many Christian churches as the first official celebration of the Resurrection of Jesus. Historically, it is during this service that people are baptized and that adult catechumens are received into full communion with the Church. It is held in the hours of darkness between sunset on Holy Saturday and sunrise on Easter Day—most commonly in the evening of Holy Saturday - but is considered to be the first celebration of Easter Day, since the Christian tradition considers feasts to begin at sunset of the previous day. The Easter Vigil has enjoyed a substantial revival among the Lutherans, having been abandoned at the Reformation.

Some churches prefer to keep this vigil very early on the Sunday morning instead of the Saturday night, particularly Protestant churches, to reflect the gospel account of the women coming to the tomb at dawn on the first day of the week. These services are known as the Sunrise service and often occur in outdoor setting such as the church's yard or a nearby park or a cemetery.

Easter Sunday – Begin Easter Week or Octave of Easter

On Easter morning some women and apostles went to Jesus' tomb, expecting to find his body. But the tomb was empty, and the angel at the tomb told them, *"He is not here; he has risen!"* Later they saw their risen Lord face to face. The gospels record these events, but the earliest written report concerning the resurrection of Jesus Christ was written by St. Paul within twenty-five years of Christ's death in 1 Corinthians 15:3-8: *"For what I received I passed on to you as of first importance: that Christ died for our sins according to the Scriptures, that he was buried, that he was raised on the third day according to the Scriptures, and that he appeared to Peter and then to the Twelve. After that, he appeared to more than five hundred of the brothers at the same time, most of whom are still living, though some have fallen asleep."*

Later St. Luke the historian wrote in his introduction to the book of Acts, *"After [Jesus'] suffering, he showed himself to these men and gave many convincing proofs that he was alive. He appeared to them over a period of forty days and spoke about the kingdom of God"* (Acts 1:3).

We cannot deny the Evangelists' agreement as to the fact that the risen Christ appeared to one or more persons. According to Matthew, He appeared to the women, and again on a mountain in Galilee; according to Mark, He was seen by Mary Magdalene, by the two disciples at Emmaus, and the Eleven of His disciples before his Ascension into heaven; according to Luke, He walked with the disciples to Emmaus, appeared to Peter and to the assembled disciples in Jerusalem; according to John, Jesus appeared to Mary Magdalene, to the ten Apostles on Easter Sunday, to the Eleven a week later, and to the seven disciples at the Sea of Tiberius. Paul in 1 Corinthians 15:3-8 enumerates another series of appearances of Jesus after His Resurrection; he was seen by Peter, by the Eleven, by more than 500 brethren, many of whom were still alive at the time of the Apostle's writing, by James, by all the Apostles, and lastly by Paul himself. The resurrection was an historical fact that was witnessed by many people!

Easter Week is the week beginning with the Christian feast of Easter and ending a week later on Easter Saturday. Additional celebrations are usually offered on Easter Sunday itself. Typically these services follow the usual order of Sunday services in a congregation, but also typically incorporate more highly festive elements. The music of the service, in particular, often displays a highly festive tone; the incorporation of brass instruments (trumpets, etc.) to supplement a congregation's usual instrumentation is common. Often a congregation's worship space is decorated with special banners and flowers (such as Easter lilies).

Eastertide
> The season of Easter begins on Easter Sunday and lasts until the day of Pentecost, seven weeks later. Eastertide is the English term for the liturgical season immediately following Easter. The first eight days of the Eastertide are commonly referred to as the Octave of Easter. In former years, Easter, as the most important celebration in Christianity, was observed for a week. However, owing to modern working patterns, many Easter celebrations now occur on Easter Sunday and possibly Easter Monday only.

Easter Monday - Easter Saturday

Ascension Day
> The Ascension is one of the great feasts in the Christian liturgical calendar, and commemorates the bodily Ascension of Jesus into Heaven. Ascension Day is

officially celebrated on a Thursday, the fortieth day of Eastertide.

The observance of this feast is of great antiquity. Although no documentary evidence of it exists prior to the beginning of the fifth century, St. Augustine says that it is of Apostolic origin, and he speaks of it in a way that shows it was the universal observance of the Church long before his time. Frequent mention of it is made in the writings of the church Fathers. The *Pilgrimage of Aetheria* speaks of the vigil of this feast and of the feast itself, as they were kept in the church built over the grotto in Bethlehem in which Christ was born.

Pentecost

Pentecost is one of the prominent feasts in the Christian liturgical year, celebrated the fiftieth day after Easter Sunday. Historically and symbolically related to the Jewish harvest festival of Shavuot, it commemorates the descent of the Holy Spirit upon the Apostles and other followers of Jesus as described in the Book of Acts.

Christians understand Pentecost as a powerful feast of salvation, because it speaks about the giving of the Law on Mount Sinai, about the founding of the Church, and about the Final Judgement. Pentecost can be seen parallel to Shavout, is Easter is to Passover. On Passover, the Jews were delivered from slavery in Egypt; On Easter, mankind was delivered from slavery to sin. On Shavout the Children of Israel received the Law; On Pentecost, the Church received the fullness of the Holy Spirit.

Appendix Five
The 17th day in the Jewish month of Tammuz

The 17th day in the Jewish month of Tammuz, Jews the world over fast and lament to commemorate the many calamities that have befallen our people on this ominous day. The purpose of such fasts in the Jewish calendar is, according to Rabbi Eliyahu Kitov's *Book of Our Heritage*, "to awaken hearts towards repentance through recalling our forefathers' misdeeds; misdeeds which led to calamities..."

A Historic Day of Calamity
Going all the way back to Biblical times, Moses descended Mount Sinai on this day and, upon seeing the Golden Calf broke the first set of Tablets carrying the Ten Commandments (Shemot 32:19, Mishna Taanit 28b).

In the First Temple Era: The priests in the First Temple stopped offering the daily sacrifice on this day (Taanit 28b) due to the shortage of sheep during the siege and the next year 3184 (586 BCE), the walls of Jerusalem were breached after many months of siege by Nebuchadnezzar and his Babylonian forces.

In Melachim II 21:7 we find that King Menashe, one of the worst of the Jewish kings, had an idol placed in the Holy Sanctuary of the Temple, according to tradition on this date. The Talmud, in Masechet Taanit 28b, says that in the time of the Roman persecution, Apostomos, captain of the occupation forces, did the same, and publicly burned the Torah - both acts considered open blasphemy and desecration. These were followed by Titus and Rome breaching the walls of Jerusalem in 3760 (70 CE) and Pope Gregory IX ordering the confiscation of all manuscripts of the Talmud in 4999 (1239).

In later years this day continued to be a dark one for Jews. In 1391, more than 4,000 Jews were killed in Toledo and Jaen, Spain and in 4319 (1559) the Jewish Quarter of Prague was burned and looted.

The Kovno ghetto was liquidated on this day in 5704 (1944) and in 5730 (1970) Libya ordered the confiscation of Jewish property.

The Fast of the Fourth Month
The Mishna in Ta'anit 4:8 associates the 17th of Tammuz as the *"Fast of the Fourth Month"* mentioned by the prophet Zechariah. According to this Mishna, the 17th of Tammuz will be transformed in the messianic era in a day that*"shall be joy to the House of Judah"* full of *"gladness and cheerful feasts"*.

Customs
The fast of the 17th of Tammuz is observed from the break of dawn until night, one of four Jewish fasts to be observed in this manner - 3 Tishrei, 10 Tevet, 13 Adar and 17 of Tammuz. Expecting or nursing mothers and those who are ill are expected to observe the fast but with lenience, refraining from meat, luxurious food and hard liquor. Minors that are old enough to understand, though exempt from fasting, should also be fed only simple foods as a manner of education. Unlike the two Jewish fast days Yom Kippur and Tisha B'Av, washing and wearing leather are permitted on this day.

Special prayers are added to the morning and afternoon prayers. This day is the beginning of the Three Weeks, an annual period of mourning over the destruction of the first and second Temples in Jerusalem.

Appendix Six
Leviticus 25 – The Sabbatical and Jubilee Years

1 The LORD said to Moses on Mount Sinai, 2 "Speak to the Israelites and say to them: 'When you enter the land I am going to give you, the land itself must observe a Sabbath to the LORD. 3 For six years sow your fields, and for six years prune your vineyards and gather their crops. 4 But in the seventh year the land is to have a Sabbath of rest, a Sabbath to the LORD. Do not sow your fields or prune your vineyards. 5 Do not reap what grows of itself or harvest the grapes of your untended vines. The land is to have a year of rest. 6 Whatever the land yields during the Sabbath year will be food for you—for yourself, your manservant and maidservant, and the hired worker and temporary resident who live among you, 7 as well as for your livestock and the wild animals in your land. Whatever the land produces may be eaten.

The Year of Jubilee
8 " 'Count off seven Sabbaths of years—seven times seven years—so that the

seven Sabbaths of years amount to a period of forty-nine years. 9 Then have the trumpet sounded everywhere on the tenth day of the seventh month; on the Day of Atonement sound the trumpet throughout your land. 10 Consecrate the fiftieth year and proclaim liberty throughout the land to all its inhabitants. It shall be a jubilee for you; each one of you is to return to his family property and each to his own clan. 11 The fiftieth year shall be a jubilee for you; do not sow and do not reap what grows of itself or harvest the untended vines. 12 For it is a jubilee and is to be holy for you; eat only what is taken directly from the fields.

13 " 'In this Year of Jubilee everyone is to return to his own property. 14 " 'If you sell land to one of your countrymen or buy any from him, do not take advantage of each other. 15 You are to buy from your countryman on the basis of the number of years since the Jubilee. And he is to sell to you on the basis of the number of years left for harvesting crops. 16 When the years are many, you are to increase the price, and when the years are few, you are to decrease the price, because what he is really selling you is the number of crops. 17 Do not take advantage of each other, but fear your God. I am the LORD your God.

18 " 'Follow my decrees and be careful to obey my laws, and you will live safely in the land. 19 Then the land will yield its fruit, and you will eat your fill and live there in safety. 20 You may ask, "What will we eat in the seventh year if we do not plant or harvest our crops?" 21 I will send you such a blessing in the sixth year that the land will yield enough for three years. 22 While you plant during the eighth year, you will eat from the old crop and will continue to eat from it until the harvest of the ninth year comes in.
23 " 'The land must not be sold permanently, because the land is mine and you are but aliens and my tenants. 24 Throughout the country that you hold as a possession, you must provide for the redemption of the land.

25 " 'If one of your countrymen becomes poor and sells some of his property, his nearest relative is to come and redeem what his countryman has sold. 26 If, however, a man has no one to redeem it for him but he himself prospers and acquires sufficient means to redeem it, 27 he is to determine the value for the years since he sold it and refund the balance to the man to whom he sold it; he can then go back to his own property. 28 But if he does not acquire the means to repay him, what he sold will remain in the possession of the buyer until the Year of Jubilee. It will be returned in the Jubilee, and he can then go back to his property.

29 " 'If a man sells a house in a walled city, he retains the right of redemption a full year after its sale. During that time he may redeem it. 30 If it is not redeemed before a full year has passed, the house in the walled city shall belong permanently to the buyer and his descendants. It is not to be returned in the Jubilee. 31 But houses in villages without walls around them are to be considered as open country. They can be redeemed, and they are to be returned in the Jubilee.

32 " 'The Levites always have the right to redeem their houses in the Levitical towns, which they possess. 33 So the property of the Levites is redeemable—that is, a house sold in any town they hold—and is to be returned in the Jubilee, because the houses in the towns of the Levites are their property among the Israelites. 34 But the

pastureland belonging to their towns must not be sold; it is their permanent possession.
35 " 'If one of your countrymen becomes poor and is unable to support himself among you, help him as you would an alien or a temporary resident, so he can continue to live among you. 36 Do not take interest of any kind [a] from him, but fear your God, so that your countryman may continue to live among you. 37 You must not lend him money at interest or sell him food at a profit. 38 I am the LORD your God, who brought you out of Egypt to give you the land of Canaan and to be your God.

39 " 'If one of your countrymen becomes poor among you and sells himself to you, do not make him work as a slave. 40 He is to be treated as a hired worker or a temporary resident among you; he is to work for you until the Year of Jubilee. 41 Then he and his children are to be released, and he will go back to his own clan and to the property of his forefathers. 42 Because the Israelites are my servants, whom I brought out of Egypt, they must not be sold as slaves. 43 Do not rule over them ruthlessly, but fear your God.

44 " 'Your male and female slaves are to come from the nations around you; from them you may buy slaves. 45 You may also buy some of the temporary residents living among you and members of their clans born in your country, and they will become your property. 46 You can will them to your children as inherited property and can make them slaves for life, but you must not rule over your fellow Israelites ruthlessly.

47 " 'If an alien or a temporary resident among you becomes rich and one of your countrymen becomes poor and sells himself to the alien living among you or to a member of the alien's clan, 48 he retains the right of redemption after he has sold himself. One of his relatives may redeem him: 49 An uncle or a cousin or any blood relative in his clan may redeem him. Or if he prospers, he may redeem himself. 50 He and his buyer are to count the time from the year he sold himself up to the Year of Jubilee. The price for his release is to be based on the rate paid to a hired man for that number of years. 51 If many years remain, he must pay for his redemption a larger share of the price paid for him. 52 If only a few years remain until the Year of Jubilee, he is to compute that and pay for his redemption accordingly. 53 He is to be treated as a man hired from year to year; you must see to it that his owner does not rule over him ruthlessly.

54 " 'Even if he is not redeemed in any of these ways, he and his children are to be released in the Year of Jubilee, 55 for the Israelites belong to me as servants. They are my servants, whom I brought out of Egypt. I am the LORD your God.

Appendix Seven
A Modern Day Miracle of the Sabbath year

The Seventh Year
My name is Dov Weiss, and I was one of a group of about thirty young men that started the *moshav* (agricultural settlement) of Komemiyut, in the south of Israel. It was in 1950, after we had completed our army service. I was still a bachelor then. Among the founders was also the well known Torah scholar and rabbinical authority, Rabbi Benyamin Mendelson, of blessed memory. He had previously immigrated to Israel from

Poland and had served as the rabbi of Kfar Ata.

At first we lived in tents, in the middle of a barren wilderness. The nearest settlements to ours were several kibbutzim associated with the left-wing *Shomer Hatzair* movement: Gat, Gilon, and Negvah. Several of our members supported themselves by working at Kibbutz Gat, the closest to us, doing different types of manual labor. Others worked in our fields, planting wheat, barley, rye and other grains and legumes. I myself drove a tractor. Our produce, which grew throughout the 15,000 or so *dunam* (nearly 4000 acres) allotted us, we sold to bakeries and factories.

At that time, there were not yet water pipes reaching our *moshav*. We had to content ourselves with what could be grown in dry rugged fields. Every few days we would make a trip to Kibbutz Negvah, about 20 kilometers distant, to fill large containers with drinking water.

The second year we were there, 5711 on the Jewish calendar (1950-1951), was the *shmitah* year which comes every seventh year in which the Torah commands to desist from all agricultural work. We were among the very few settlements in Israel at the time to observe the laws of the Sabbatical year and refrain from working the land. Instead, we concentrated on building and succeeded that year in completing much of the permanent housing. The *moshav* gradually developed and expanded and more and more families moved in, as well as a number of young singles. By the end of the year we numbered around eighty people.

As the Sabbatical year drew to its completion we prepared to renew our farming activities. For this we required seed to sow crops, but for this purpose we could only use wheat from the sixth year, the year that preceded the *shmitah*, for the produce of the seventh year is forbidden for this type of use. We went around to all the agricultural settlements in the area, near and far, seeking good quality seed from the previous years' harvest, but no one could fulfill our request.

All we were able to find was some old wormy seed that, for reasons that were never made clear to us, was laying around in a storage shed in Kibbutz Gat. No farmer in his right mind anywhere in the world would consider using such poor quality seed to plant with, not if he expected to see any crops from it. The kibbutzniks at Gat all burst into loud derisive laughter when we revealed that we were actually interested in this infested grain that had been rotting away for a few years in some dark, murky corner. "If you really want it, you can take all that you like, and for free, with our compliments," they offered in amusement.

We consulted with Rabbi Mendelson. His response was: "Take it. The One who tells wheat to sprout from good seed can also order it to grow from inferior wormy leftover seed as well." In any case, we didn't have an alternative. So we loaded all the old infested seed that the kibbutz had offered to us free of charge onto a tractor and returned to Komemiyut.

The laws of *shemittah* forbade us to plough and turn over the soil till after Rosh Hashanah, the beginning of the eighth year, so we didn't actually sow the seed until

93

until sometime in November. This was two or three months after all the other farmers had already completed their planting.

That year, the rains were late in coming. The farmers from all the *kibbutzim* and *moshavim* gazed upward longingly for the first rain. They began to feel desperate, but the heavens were unresponsive, remaining breathlessly still and blue.

Finally it rained. When? The day after we completed planting our thousand *dunam* of wheat fields with those wormy seeds, the sky opened up and the rains exploded down to saturate the parched earth.

The following days we were nervous in anticipation but we turned our attention to strengthening our faith and trust in G-d. Anyway, it did not take a long time for the hand of the Al-mighty to be revealed clearly to all. Those wheat fields that were planted during the seventh year, months before the first rain, sprouted only small weak crops. At the same time, our fields, sowed with the old infested seed and long after the appropriate season, were covered with an unusually large and healthy yield of wheat, in comparison to any standard.

The story of "the miracle at Komemiyut" spread quickly. Farmers from all the agricultural settlements in the region came to see with their own eyes what they could not believe when they heard the rumors about it. When the farmers from Kibbutz Gat arrived, they pulled a surprise on us. After absorbing the sight of the bountiful quantity of wheat flourishing in our fields, they announced they wanted payment for the tractor-load of old rotten wheat they had scornfully given us for free only a short time before. Even more startling: they said they would file a claim against us at a *beit din*, a rabbinical court, and with Rabbi Mendelson himself, no less! They must have figured that in a secular court such a claim wouldn't have even the slightest possible chance of gaining them a single penny.

Rabbi Mendelson accepted their case seriously, and in the end judged that we should pay them. He explained that the reason they gave it for free was because they thought it worthless for planting, while in truth it really was excellent for that purpose. We were astonished to hear his ruling, but needless to say, we complied.

The whole story became an extraordinary *kiddush Hashem* (glorification of G-d) in the eyes of Jews across the country. Everyone agreed it was a clear fulfillment of G-d's promise in the Torah (Leviticus 25): *Six years you shall sow your field, and six years you shall prune your vineyard, and gather in its fruit. But in the seventh year shall be a sabbath of solemn rest for the land, a sabbath for G-d...And if you shall say: "What shall we eat in the seventh year? Behold, we shall not sow, nor gather in our produce!" But I will command my blessing upon you...*

Editor's note:

Today, Komemiyut is world famous for its high-quality *shmurah matzah* (lit. "matzah that has been watched") -- round, hand-made matzah prepared under exacting supervision from the time the wheat is harvested through the end of the baking to guard against the minutest moisture.

Appendix Eight
Fill Out Pruzbul

This upcoming year, 5768, is a *Shmitah* (Sabbatical) year. Part of the observance of *Shmitah* includes the forgiving of loans. More than 2000 years ago, loans and money flow slowed as the *Shmitah* year neared. Rather than have the economy slow down, Hillel the Elder instituted the *pruzbul* system. The Torah states that all private debts are forgiven, public debts are exempt. The act of *pruzbul* makes private debts public and therefore redeemable.

The *pruzbul* can be done orally before three adult men who constitute a court. One approaches this "court" and states that he/she is transferring to them all debts which may are owed to him/her, thus making them collectable. This must be done before Rosh Hashanah.

If this option is not available to you, fill out the form below before early afternoon of Wednesday, September 12, and fax it to 718-467-3263 or email it to Services@Chabadonline.com

I, the undersigned, transfer to you, Rabbis Schapiro, Schochet and Sharfstein, all debts that are owed me, in writing or verbally, so that I may collect them at any time I desire.
Date:_____
Signature: _____

Appendix Nine
Battles of the Maccabean Revolt

There were a number of key battles between the Maccabees and the Seleucid Syrian-Greeks:
   Battle of Adasa (Judas Maccabeus leads the Jews to victory against the forces of
      Nicanor.)
   Battle of Beth Horon (Judas Maccabeus defeats the forces of Seron.)
   Battle of Beth Zur (Judas Maccabeus defeats the army of Lysias, recapturing
      Jerusalem.)
   Battle of Beth-zechariah (Elazar the Maccabee is killed in battle. Lysias has success
      in battle against the Maccabess, but allows them temporary freedom of worship.)
   Battle of Emmaus (Judas Maccabeus fights the forces of Lysias and Georgias).
   Dathema (A Jewish fortress saved by Judas Maccabeus.)
   Battle of Elasa (Judas Maccabeus dies in battle against the army of King Demetrius
      and Bacchides. He is succeeded by Jonathan Maccabaeus and Simon
      Maccabaeus who continue to lead the Jews in battle.)

Appendix Ten
The Hasmonean Kingdom

198 BCE: Armies of the Seleucid King Antiochus III (Antiochus the Great) oust Ptolemy V from Judea and Samaria.

175 BCE: Antiochus IV (Epiphanes) ascends the Seleucid throne.

168 BCE: Under the reign of Antiochus IV, the Temple is looted, Jews are massacred, and Judaism is outlawed.

167 BCE: Antiochus orders an altar to Zeus erected in the Temple. Mattathias, and his five sons John, Simon, Eleazar, Jonathan, and Judah lead a rebellion against Antiochus. Judah becomes known as Judah Maccabe (Judah The Hammer).

166 BCE: Mattathias dies, and Judah takes his place as leader. The Hasmonean Jewish Kingdom begins; It lasts until 63 BCE

165 BCE: The Jewish revolt against the Seleucid monarchy is successful. The Temple is liberated and rededicated (Hanukkah).

142 BCE: Establishment of the Second Jewish Commonwealth. The Seleucids recognize Jewish autonomy. The Seleucid kings have a formal overlordship, which the Hasmoneans acknowledged. This inaugurates a period of great geographical expansion, population growth, and religious, cultural and social development.

139 BCE: The Roman Senate recognizes Jewish autonomy.

130 BCE: Antiochus VII besieges Jerusalem, but withdraws.

131 BCE: Antiochus VII dies. The Hasmonean Jewish Kingdom throws off Syrian rule completely

96 BCE: An eight year civil war begins.

83 BCE: Consolidation of the Kingdom in territory east of the Jordan River.

63 BCE: The Hasmonean Jewish Kingdom comes to an end due to rivalry between the brothers Aristobulus II and Hyrcanus II, both of whom appeal to the Roman Republic to intervene and settle the power struggle on their behalf. The Roman general Gnaeus Pompeius Magnus (Pompey the Great) is dispatched to the area. Twelve thousand Jews are massacred as Romans enter Jerusalem. The Priests of the Temple are struck down at the Altar. Rome annexes Judea.

Bibliography

Samuele Bacchiocchi. *From Sabbath To Sunday*. Rome, Italy; The Pontifical Gregorian University Press, 1977 – 369 pages.
> An historical investigation of the rise of Sunday observance in Early Christianity.

Richard and Michele Berkowitz. *Shabbat*. Baltimore, Maryland; Lederer Publications, 1983 – 46 pages.
> A Messianic Jewish Sabbath Celebration.

Philip Birnbaum. *High Holiday Prayer Book*. New York, New York, Hebrew Publishing Company, 1951.
> This is the prayer book of the festivals revealing a rich anthology of Israel's literary classics showing the sorrows and joys of the Jewish people. These are metrical compositions that were inspired by the synagogue services.

Arlene Cardozo. *Jewish Family Celebrations*. New York, NY; St. Martin's Press, 1982 – 259 pages.
> This is a lively guide through the calendar year of Jewish observance for families seeking to incorporate Jewish heritage into their lives.

Earl and Alice Count. *4000 Years of Christmas*. Berkley, CA.; Ulysses Press, 1997 – 103 pages.
> The history of Christmas traditions and where they came from.

William Curtis. *The Forgotten Feast*. Columbus, GA.; Brentwood Christian Press,1985 – 62 pages.
> This small book shows the redemptive plan of God through the feasts of Israel.

Abba Eben. *The Story of the Jews*. New York, New York, Behrman House Inc., 1968 – 534 Pages.
> A book to explain the Jewish people to a "confused and often uncomprehending world."

Philip Goodman. *The Purim Anthology*. Jerusalem, Israel, The Jewish Publication Society, 1949 – 526 Pages.
> An anthology filled with all the sources and resources that a family needs to understand and celebrate the Jewish holidays and holy days. This book interprets the holiday cycle.

Frederick C. Grant. *Ancient Judaism and The New Testament*. New York, New York, The McMillan Company, 1959 – 155 Pages.
> The treasures of Judaism's historic faith are seen to be the antecedent to Christian sacred literature and life.

Isidor Grunfeld. *Shemittah and Yobel: Laws referring to the Sabbatical Year in Israel and Its Produce.* Jerusalem, Israel, The Soncino Press, 1972 – 151 pages.
> This book is on the dietary laws of the Israel specifically connected to the various festival occasions.

Robert Hamerton-Kelly. *Spring Time: Seasons of the Christian Year.* Nashville, TN.; The Upper Room, 1980 – 144 pages.
> This book explains the main themes of the Christian year and reveals what the Scriptures teach us about these events.

E.W. Hengstenberg. *The Christology of the Old Testament.* Grand Rapids, Michigan, Kregel Publications, 1970 – 715 Pages.
> This books shows us all the places in the Old Testament that teach, show or reveal   Christ to us.

Hans Holzer. *Star in the East.* New York, New York; Pyramid Books, 1972 – 95 pages.
> His book seeks to discover how much of the Christmas story is actually true.

Betty Howard. *God's Gift of Love.* Orlando, Fl.; The Good News Connection, Inc., 2001 – 113 pages.
> This is the story of Mary and Elizabeth and the birth of their sons.

Barney Kasdan. *God's Appointed Times.* Baltimore, Maryland; Lederer Messianic Publications, 1993 – 136 pages.
> This book shows the historical background of the Jewish feasts and how Christians can celebrate them also.

Alfred J. Kolatch. *The Jewish Book of Why.* Middle Village, NY, Jonathan David Publishers, Inc., 1995 – 325 pages.
> This is a book that answers why Jewish people believe and practice the things they do.

Thomas Lawler. *St Augustine: Sermons for Christmas and Epiphany.* New York, NY; Newman Press, 1952 – 231 pages.
> This is a collection of all of St. Augustine's sermons on Christmas and Epiphany.

Max Lucado. *And the Angels Were Silent.* Sisters, Oregon; Multnomah Publishers, 1992 – 263 pages.
> This book is on the subject of the final week of Jesus life before the crucifixion.

John MacArthur, Jr. *God With Us: The Miracle of Christmas.* Grand Rapids, MI., Zondervan Books, 1989 – 134 pages.

Chaim Raphael. *Festival Days, A History of Jewish Celebrations.* New York, New York, Grove Weidenfeld, 1990 – 144 Pages
> A demonstration of the uniqueness of Jewish history in the world story.

Robin Sampson, Linda Pierce. *A Family Guide to the Biblical Holidays.* Stafford, Va., Heart of Wisdom Publishing, Inc., 1997 - 583 pages.
> This is a book of family teaching and activities in celebrating the feasts and festivals of the Bible and of God's people.

Nosson Scherman and Meir Zlotowitz. *Chanukah.* Brooklyn, New York; Mesorah Publications, Ltd., 1989 - 159 pages.
> The history, observance and significance of Chanukah based on the Talmudic and traditional sources.

Arthur Stanley. *Lectures on the History of the Jewish Church Vols. I & II.* New York, New York, Charles Scribner and Company, 1871 – 1228 Pages.
> This book is a series of lectures designed to delineate the outward events of the sacred history to bring out their inward spirit that the more complete realization of their outward form should not denigrate but exalt the Faith of which they are the vehicle.

William Whiston. *The Works of Flavius Josephus.* Grand Rapids, Michigan, Associated Publishers and Authors, Inc.
> This work is regarded as the only reference in history containing valid contemporary references to Christ. This book offers detailed accounts of Jewish life in the first century.

Dick York. *The Other side of the Christmas Tree.* San Antonio, Texas; Dick York, 1990 – 105 pages.
> This book is essentially teaching that the celebration of Christmas and other non-biblical holidays violate the Scriptures.

Made in the USA
Columbia, SC
01 June 2024

36383369R00057